Reshaping the Future

Reshaping the Future

Education and Postconflict Reconstruction

THE WORLD BANK
Washington, D.C.

Contents

BOXES

Acknowledgments

This study was undertaken by a small team in the Human Development Network Education Hub (HDNED) under the leadership of Peter Buckland, Senior Education Specialist, who would like to acknowledge the important contribution of Raymond Muhula, Research Assistant. His relentless pursuit of data in a very challenging context provided important basic information for this study. The work would not have been undertaken without the support of HDNED. Sector Director, Ruth Kagia, and the steadfast and expert guidance and encouragement of the Education Sector Manager, Jamil Salmi. The work of the team was supported by regular comments and inputs from a wide range of people in the Bank, most of whom were members of a small community of practice groups established for the purpose. Key among them were Ian Bannon, Ernesto Cuadra, Peter Colenso, Tia Duer, Kuzvinetsa Dzvimbo, Vince Greaney, Rick Hopper, Maureen Lewis, Saida Mamedova, Juan Moreno, Susan Opper, Bob Prouty, Francis Steier, Gary Theisen, Chris Thomas, Eluned Roberts-Schweitzer, and Jim Stevens. Also acknowledged here is the valuable contribution of the external reviewers, Nat Colletta and Marc Sommers. The work of the team was ably supported throughout by colleagues in the Education Advisory Service and by Inosha Wickramasekera and Mado Ndau, who provided invaluable help with logistical arrangements.

Foreword

Violent conflict, with its bloody assault on people and institutions and its invariably debilitating aftermath, is the epitome of "development in reverse." Sadly, as the many case studies in this book and other publications amply demonstrate, conflict and poverty are closely interwoven. Conflict blunts, and subsequently unravels, years of hard-won economic and social development. Recent research also shows us that development patterns—which worsen inequalities, deepen poverty, or slash at the ties that bind societies together—can themselves contribute to the likelihood of conflict and its haunting recurrence.

One of the most devastating impacts of violent conflict is the damage it inflicts on education systems and the children and students they serve. More than two million children have died as a direct result of armed conflict over the last decade. At least six million children have been seriously injured or permanently disabled. Long after the guns stop firing, the lives of students and teachers continue to be imperiled by the discarded litter of war: landmines, unexploded shells, and the proliferation of assault rifles, guns, and ammunition. Some schools in Cambodia and Angola will be closed for years to come because they sit in the middle of a minefield, and whole villages have simply become "no-go" areas.

Teachers often bear a heavy cost in times of conflict. In Rwanda more than two-thirds of the teachers in primary and secondary schools were killed or fled. In Cambodia the carnage was even greater, leaving the system virtually without trained or experienced teachers. In Timor Leste, the impact on teacher numbers of that relatively short conflict was uneven: in primary schools, 80 percent of the teachers were Timorese and remained, while almost all secondary school teachers were Indonesian. The failure of the Indonesian teachers to return left Timor

Leste with almost no trained or qualified personnel for its secondary system and no access to tertiary education.

These effects ravage the education process. They also constitute a formidable roadblock for the efforts of poor countries to achieve the Education for All (EFA) Millennium Development Goals, especially the 2015 targets of universal primary school completion and gender equality in primary and secondary education. The central message of this book is that education has a key role in both preventing conflict and rebuilding fractured postconflict societies.

Education commands high priority in both the initial humanitarian phase of national and international response and in the postconflict rebuilding phase. Every education system has the potential to either aggravate the conditions that lead to violent conflict or to heal them. The unavoidable conclusion must be that ignoring education, or postponing it, is not an option.

Even when it is part of a humanitarian response, education is a development activity and must be undertaken with a developmental perspective if it is to contribute to reversing the damage and to building resilience to prevent further violent conflict.

Yet schools and education systems, whether they were a contributory factor to a conflict, are invariably debilitated by conflict. They are left weakened, damaged, and underresourced at precisely the time when communities, governments, and international agencies need them to help rebuild and transform themselves and the societies they serve. This twin mandate of reform and reconstruction offers both significant opportunities and enormous challenges to societies emerging from conflict.

The outpouring of analysis, publications, and research projects in this field in the past two years suggests that there is now strong recognition of the importance of early investment in education as a prerequisite for successful postconflict reconstruction.

Jean-Louis Sarbib
Senior Vice President
Human Development Network
World Bank

Jamil Salmi
Acting Sector Director
Department of Education
Human Development Network
World Bank

Acronyms and Abbreviations

ADB	Asian Development Bank
CAF	Conflict Analysis Framework
CIDA	Canadian International Development Agency
CSO	Civil society organization
EDUCA	Education with Community Participation Program
EFA	Education for All
EMIS	Education Management Information Systems
EQUIP	Education Quality Improvement Project
GDP	Gross Domestic Product
GER	Gross Enrollment Rate
GoSL	Government of Sri Lanka
HPIC	Heavily Indebted Poor Countries
IBE	International Bureau for Education
IDA	International Development Association
LICUS	Low Income Countries Under Stress
LTTE	Liberation Tigers of Tamil Eelam
NGO	Nongovernmental organization
NATO	North Atlantic Treaty Organization
MDG	Millennium Development Goals
MPLA	Popular Movement for the Liberation of Angola
PNA	Preliminary Needs Assessment
PRSP	Poverty Reduction Strategy Paper
REBEP	Rehabilitation of Basic Education Project
TSS	Transportation Support Strategies
UPC	Universal Primary Completion
UNAMSIL	United Nations Mission in Sierra Leone
UNESCO	United Nations Educational, Scientific and Cultural Organization

UNECO IIEP	International Institute for Educational Planning (UNESCO)
UNHCR	United Nations High Commissioner for Refugees
UNICEF	United Nations Children's Fund
UNITA	National Union for the Total Independence of Angola
UNMIK	United Nations Mission in Kosovo
UNTAET	United Nations Transitional Administration in East Timor

Executive Summary

The relationship between education systems and conflict presents policymakers with a conundrum. Schools are almost always complicit in conflict. They reproduce the skills, values, attitudes, and social relations of dominant groups in society; accordingly, they are usually a contributory factor in conflict. Simultaneously reconstructing and reforming education is increasingly viewed as a critical element in the strategy to reduce the risk of conflict or relapse into conflict. The central message of this paper, therefore, is that conflict presents not only challenges for reconstruction but also significant opportunities for reform of education systems. The challenge of simultaneous reform and reconstruction at a time of constrained human, financial, and institutional resources and considerable urgency calls for particular attention to priorities and sequencing of interventions. Short-term immediate responses need to be conceptualized within a framework that provides for more substantial systemic reform as the new political vision emerges and system capacity is built.

Conflict, which has been conceptualized as "development in reverse,"[1] should be analyzed in the context of its impact on development. Reducing poverty and decreasing reliance on primary commodity exports, both of which require a functioning and effective education system, have been shown to be critical strategies for reducing the risk of conflict. Ethnic or religious dominance rather than diversity is also a powerful contributory factor in civil conflict; education has a key role in mediating or deepening ethnic, religious, and other identity-based conflicts. Civil war itself increases the likelihood of further outbreaks of conflict. Education that helps to build stronger resilience to conflict is therefore a critical strategy for post-conflict reconstruction.

Conflict has a devastating impact on education, both directly in terms of the suffering and psychological impact on the pupils, teachers, and communities, and in the degradation of the education system and its infrastructure. Yet these same education systems are expected to make a significant contribution to rebuilding a shattered society at a time when they themselves are debilitated by the effects of conflict. Fortunately, as this study demonstrates, schools and education systems are surprisingly resilient, and the disruption caused by conflict offers opportunities as well as challenges for social reconstruction.

The paper offers an overview of the key findings of a study of education and postconflict reconstruction and draws on a literature review, a database of key indicators for 52 conflict-affected countries, and a review of 12 country studies.

Reform and Reconstruction

The challenges that postconflict reconstruction of education faces, which are very much the same as those faced by all education systems struggling with reform, are complicated by an added sense of urgency and the additional debilitating aftereffects of war. Four factors identified in a recent set of case studies of education reform are just as critical in postconflict societies:

- Sound policies and committed leadership at the country level
- Adequate operational capacity at all levels, including capacity of communities to participate effectively, with the right incentives
- Financial resources to scale up programs that work and ensure these reach the service delivery level
- A relentless focus on results.

These are demanding requirements in any circumstances, but they are no less critical for reform and reconstruction in postconflict societies. The lesson from successful initiatives is that each of these factors should be approached in an iterative manner. The "relentless focus on results," for instance, may start with simply ensuring the measuring and reporting of results in terms of visible impact—books delivered or schools repaired, or increased access and equity—while the system restores its capacity to measure the real results of reform: the impact on learning outcomes.

All this must be achieved in a context where political authority and civil administration are often weakened, compromised, or inexperienced; civil society is in disarray, deeply divided, and more familiar with the politics of opposition than reconstruction; financial resources are constrained and unpredictable. Yet each of these constraints also contains possibilities: new political authorities are more likely to seek education reform to distance themselves from the previous regime, particularly where international aid provides additional incentives. Weakened bureaucracies are less able to resist reform. Civil society often focuses on education as a key strategy around which it can coalesce for reform, and the publicity around the end of conflict often attracts an injection of resources that can help to kick-start reform.

In this situation where the demands on an education system frequently outstrip its capacity to deliver, the question of priorities looms large. In facing challenges on all fronts, where does one begin? This study suggests four important starting points:

- First, focus on the basics to get the system functioning so that the return of children and youth to school can be seen as an early "peace dividend" that will help to shore up support for peace.
- Second, acknowledge the importance of symbolism in education and ensure some bold symbolic actions (such as purging textbooks) signaling that, while much about the system remains unchanged, the reform has started.
- Third, build recognition that reform of education is an incremental and ongoing process that takes decades and must be led from within the country as consensus develops on the wider development vision of that society.
- Fourth, focus from the beginning on building capacity for reform, which includes supporting the participation of communities, local authorities, and other stakeholders.

Some other important overarching lessons that emerged from the study are as follows:

- Make use of interim arrangements and transitional mechanisms.
- Prioritize basic education within a system-wide approach.
- Demonstrate early and visible impact.
- Decentralize the system to encourage parental involvement in school governance.
- Build the capacity of the central authorities to ensure an enabling environment for decentralization.
- Build effective partnerships and work closely with interagency coordination mechanisms.
- Recognize the contribution that returning refugees, and especially youth, can make to the process of education reconstruction.

Teachers, Reform, and Reconstruction

Teachers are the most critical resource in education reconstruction. During early reconstruction, many teachers return to their previous posts along with members of communities who may have been involved in supporting education during the conflict. The education system often offers the first opportunities for public sector employment; at the same time many qualified teachers are attracted to new opportunities in the new bureaucracy, and in the international agencies and nongovernmental organizations (NGOs). This often results in a shortage of qualified teachers accompanied by oversupply of underqualified or unqualified teachers in early reconstruction. Poor recordkeeping can result in "ghost teachers," requiring rationalization of the teaching force.

Teacher development and training, largely neglected during conflict in most cases, creates particular challenges for postconflict reconstruction as the system has to respond to the training backlog, an influx of untrained teachers, and limited capacity of the central authorities to coordinate the wide range of private and donor-sponsored training initiatives. The greatest challenge for new authorities is to coordinate this energy into a more coherent teacher development program without stifling it with bureaucratic controls. Teacher organizations, which often have the potential to obstruct reform, can play a significant positive role in supporting reconstruction. The key appears to be in early involvement and ongoing dialogue.

Curriculum, Textbooks, and Reform

Curriculum and textbook reform calls for a cautious and sequential approach to ensure that guidance on key curriculum matters does not outpace development of a wider curriculum vision for the system. Curriculum reform is a major national undertaking requiring strong and clear political leadership, extensive consultations, considerable technical expertise, and comprehensive training programs for teachers. It cannot be rushed. Yet change is often unavoidable. Textbooks, which frequently exert more influence on classroom practice than official curriculum documents, are often identified as a starting point for curriculum change, especially where they are seen to reflect bias, prejudice, or distorted interpretations. Early curriculum reform may even involve decisions to eliminate some subjects from the curriculum and to incorporate new issues related to the conflict.

Governance and Financing

In terms of governance and financing, the following key lessons emerged:

- The "relief bubble" in international financial support often subsides before a more predictable flow of reconstruction resources can be mobilized.
- Corruption and transparency in education governance are an abiding concern of communities in almost all postconflict contexts.
- Early reconstruction often requires international support for recurrent as well as capital expenditure, since few countries have quick access to domestic revenue necessary to keep the system running.
- International support targeted at reconstruction of infrastructure and other capital investments is more effective when linked to longer-term sector development plans.
- Reduction of household costs of education is an effective strategy to promote access and equity, but it requires careful implementation so as not to compromise quality.

The Legacy of Conflict

In addition to the "usual business" of system reconstruction at the core of any postconflict reconstruction, the legacy of conflict brings additional challenges that derive directly from the conflict and call for creative strategies to be integrated into reconstruction programs. This includes the issue of sectoral imbalance, with a strong tendency of international agencies to focus resources and support on basic education and neglect secondary and tertiary levels. Interagency coordination emerges as a particularly challenging area despite a plethora of coordinating agencies and bodies that have been created since the confusion of post-genocide Rwanda.

While there is a considerable literature and accumulated experience on provision of education to refugees and internally displaced persons, much less is available in the way of lessons from experience on how to link the achievements of such programs into the reconstruction of national education systems.

In almost every country study there was a recognition that youth constitute not simply a potential threat to stability should they be recruited into military or criminal activity, but also an important potential resource for development and reconstruction. The main challenges that youth face in postconflict environments are similar to those faced by youth in other development contexts, except that they are often exacerbated by conflict and its aftermath. Yet there are few helpful examples of programs that successfully address the needs and aspirations of youth in postconflict societies or tap into their potential contributions to reconstruction.

A Role for the World Bank

Finally, the study reviews the role that the World Bank has played in supporting education reconstruction and suggests some directions that might make its impact more effective. These include introducing a stronger focus on prevention into its postconflict work, which still tends to concentrate heavily on transition and recovery. More active involvement in global collaboration for greater country-level coordination would build on established strengths of the Bank in sector analysis and capacity-building for reform, data collection and consolidation, and knowledge sharing. The study also suggests some elaboration of the existing Watching Brief approach used by the Bank during conflict and a greater focus on two largely neglected areas that can have a significant impact on social and economic recovery: youth and secondary education. Finally, the study argues for a more systematic focus on the private sector, training, and market aspects of education.

The nature of postconflict reconstruction is as complex and varied as the conflicts themselves, and there are no easy or simple formulae that can be applied across all contexts. However, some lessons can be distilled from the accumulated experience to suggest directions that those involved in supporting the postconflict reconstruction of education can investigate. This study is offered as a contribution to the growing debate about those lessons.

Note

1. World Bank. 2003. *Breaking the Conflict Trap: Civil War and Development Policy.* Washington, D.C.: Oxford University Press/World Bank.

CHAPTER 1

Introduction

This book, which offers an overview of the key findings of a study of education and postconflict reconstruction, draws on a literature review, a database of key indicators for 52 conflict-affected countries, and a review of 12 country studies. The countries studied vary in terms of their present conflict status and the length, intensity, and extent of conflict. Key issues at stake in the countries studied include ethnic and religious identity, politicization of education, competition for natural resources, and continuity of civil authority and civil administration.

CONFLICT[1] CONSTITUTES A MAJOR OBSTACLE to the achievement of Education for All (EFA) and the Millennium Development Goals (MDGs), especially the sector goals of universal completion of primary education and achievement of gender equality in primary and secondary education. The central message of this book is that education has a key role both in conflict prevention and in the reconstruction of postconflict societies. It warrants high priority in both humanitarian response and in postconflict reconstruction because every education system has the potential to exacerbate the conditions that contribute to violent conflict, as well as the potential to address them. Ignoring education, or postponing educational response for some later phase, is not an option.

Even when it is part of a humanitarian response, education must be undertaken with a developmental perspective if it is to contribute to reversing the damage done by conflict and to building resilience to further violent conflict. As a development activity it is frequently an underfunded component of humanitarian response.

Irrespective of whether schools and education systems were a contributory factor in a conflict, they invariably are debilitated by conflict. They are left weakened, damaged, and underresourced at precisely the time when communities, governments, and international agencies require them to play a role in rebuilding and transforming

1

themselves and the societies they serve. This twin mandate of reform and reconstruction offers both significant opportunities and enormous challenges to societies emerging from conflict. Maximizing those opportunities and managing those constraints calls for strategies that balance prioritization and sequencing in a context of depleted human and institutional resources and unpredictable financial flows.

While few now challenge the critical role of education in development, identifying what it takes to ensure that education plays an effective role in postconflict reconstruction requires a more systematic analysis of the way education, conflict, and poverty interact.

Relationship between Conflict and Poverty

Conflict and poverty are intricately interrelated. Conflict retards economic and social development and may be conceptualized as "development in reverse" (World Bank 2003). Yet recent research also demonstrates that development patterns that exacerbate inequalities or promote economic dependence, increase or deepen poverty, or undermine social cohesion may themselves contribute to the likelihood of conflict or the recurrence of conflict.

Relationship between Education and Conflict

The relationship between education and conflict is complex and multidirectional. While the damaging impact of conflict on educational systems has been well documented, the role that these systems and schooling frequently play in reproducing the attitudes, values, and social relations underlying civil conflict and violence is less well understood. Ensuring that education plays a role in reversing the damaging effects of conflict and building or rebuilding social cohesion requires a deeper analysis of the way education impacts conflict.

The impact of conflict on education systems varies very significantly with the context, and the lessons that can be drawn from the experience of other countries can only be useful if interpreted in the light of the specific conditions unique to any particular country. However, this study suggests that there is a body of relevant international experience that can help to provide a basis for setting the priorities and thinking through issues of sequencing and capacity-building.

The Present Study

This book is based on a study undertaken by a small team in the Human Development Network Education Department. The study, building on work already undertaken within the Bank and in consultation with the Conflict Prevention and Reconstruction Unit (CPRU), draws on a review of the literature, a database of 52 countries affected by conflict since 1990, and a set of country studies. The countries in the study include four that are emerging from conflict (Angola, Burundi, Sierra Leone, and Sri Lanka); three countries or territories that have emerged from conflict since 1994 (Bosnia-Herzegovina, Kosovo, and Timor Leste); and five countries that have a longer history of postconflict reconstruction (Cambodia, El Salvador, Guatemala, Lebanon, and Nicaragua). Consideration is given to how some of these lessons might apply to countries recently involved in conflict, especially Afghanistan and Iraq.

Conflict Length and Intensity.   The 12 conflict-affected countries that are the focus of this study vary significantly with regard to length and intensity of the conflict. Bosnia-Herzegovina, Kosovo, and Timor Leste experienced relatively short periods of intense conflict (one to three years), while almost all the others were affected by conflict for periods ranging from approximately one decade (Burundi, El Salvador, Nicaragua, and Sierra Leone) to two decades (Lebanon and Sri Lanka), to three decades (Angola, Cambodia, and Guatemala). The three relatively short conflicts, however, were all very intense, and in Kosovo and Timor Leste were the culmination of a decade or more of repression and resistance.

Conflict Extent.   The extent of the conflict is a key variable in understanding the relationship between education and reconstruction. In many cases, especially in extended conflicts, violence directly affects only a part of the country; in many areas education continues to function, albeit with significantly less resources, under the direction of the state–such as in the Popular Movement for the Liberation of Angola (MPLA)-controlled areas in Angola and in most of Sri Lanka. Conflict is often confined largely to rural areas, such as in Burundi and the Central American countries, leading to massive urban migration and serious congestion of urban schools. In Bosnia-Herzegovina, Cambodia, and Kosovo the intensified conflict was widespread, and many urban as well as rural schools were directly affected.

Additional Factors.   Ethnic and religious identity, politically-based struggles, and resource-fueled conflict also impact educational reconstruction. While this book does not attempt to summarize the complex network of factors that contribute to each conflict, it is clear that conflicts where ethnic identity or religion emerge as an explicit dimension of struggle (such as Bosnia-Herzegovina, Burundi, Kosovo, Sri Lanka, and Timor Leste) place particular demands on educational reconstruction, particularly with respect to language and curriculum. Politically-driven conflict had a powerful influence on reconstruction in the three Central American countries (El Salvador, Guatemala, and Nicaragua) and in Cambodia. In Angola and Sierra Leone—two conflicts that are significantly fueled by competition for control of natural resources—it is noteworthy that the rebel groups made limited attempts to ensure provision of education in the areas that fell under their control.

Continuity in civil administration and civil authority profoundly affect reconstruction. In El Salvador and Sri Lanka, for instance, the existing state authority essentially survived the conflict and was able to apply its institutional resources to policy development and system reform. In contrast, in Cambodia, Kosovo, and Timor Leste reconstruction of education had to take place in parallel with re-establishment of civil authority and civil administration. Accordingly, the pace and pattern of reform and the relationships between internal and external actors differ considerably.

Problematic Data.   Educational data for conflict-affected countries are notoriously incomplete and unreliable, and this study encountered its share of these difficulties. The official national data reported in the international databases (UNESCO Institute for Statistics, World Bank EdStats) are particularly incomplete in the case of conflict countries, with many data gaps in the official tables even for the most basic information on enrollment, repetition, and dropout. The accuracy and reliability of the reported data have been questioned; on a number of occasions the data differ significantly from other official data available from the country or in World Bank reports that frequently draw on survey data to provide more up-to-date estimates. This makes cross-national comparisons of data problematic. In the cases of Angola and Burundi, for instance, there are documented accounts of officials continuing to report enrollment and teachers in areas where public schools no longer exist or have ceased to function (Chauterie 2000). Conversely, the unofficial nature of many educational initiatives in conflict and early reconstruction means that they are often underreported. A further complicating factor is that official data are often not disaggregated by region and district, so that the effect of conflict is masked by national averages.

This study is undertaken in a context of a significant growth in the literature in the field of education and conflict. The work builds on the recent World Bank study, "Children and War," (Sommers 2002) and on a range of recent publications emanating from the Bank that look more broadly at the issue of reconstruction and development.[2] A number of multilateral and bilateral development organizations have recently published studies and documents that examine various aspects of the relationship between education and emergencies, including conflict.[3] In addition, practical guidelines or field guidance notes that focus on field operations have also been published recently or are nearing publication, including those from the United Nations Educational, Scientific and Cultural Organization (UNESCO 2002a, b), the International Institute for Educational Planning (UNESCO IIEP), Save the Children (Nicolai and Triplehorn 2003), the United Nations Children's Fund (UNICEF forthcoming), and the United Nations High Commissioner for Refugees (UNHCR 2003). With the exception of Smith and Vaux (2003), Sinclair (2003), and the recently published IIEP monographs, most of these publications focus heavily on the emergency response phase and much less on postconflict reconstruction, although all stress the importance of a developmental approach and of continuity between emergency response and reconstruction.

Building on the existing work and on work underway in UNESCO IIEP and the International Bureau for Education (IBE), this study focuses specifically on the challenge of postconflict reconstruction and its linkages to social and economic reconstruction, social cohesion rebuilding, and conflict prevention. It offers a digest of key issues supported by specific examples to guide policymakers and practitioners, identifies a number of neglected areas that warrant more systematic focus, and suggests some priority areas for the World Bank in the immediate future.

Endnotes

1. The term "conflict" is used to refer to violent conflict including civil and interstate wars and armed rebellions.
2. For example, OP2.30 Operational Policies: Development Cooperation and Conflict (2001); or Kreimer and others (1998); and, of course, "Post Conflict Reconstruction: The Role of the World Bank" (1998), World Bank, Washington, D.C. See also reports to the Development Committee on "Assistance to Post-Conflict Countries and the HIPC Framework" (2001) and "Review of the PRSP Approach" (2002:10–11).

3. See, for example, Smith and Vaux (2003); Pigozzi (2000); Nicolai and Triplehorn (2003); Bush and Saltarelli (2000); see also recent publications from the Norwegian Refugee Council (NRC).

References

Bush, K., and Saltarelli D., eds. 2000. 'Two Faces of Education in Ethnic Conflict." Innocenti Insight." UNICEF: Florence, Italy.

Chanterie, F. 2000. "JRS Education in Cazombo." *Bulletin of the Jesuit Centre for Theological Reflection (JCTR)* No 45, pp. 1–4.

Kreimer, A., J. Eriksson, M. Arnold, and C. Scott. 1998. "The World Bank's Experience with Post-Conflict Reconstruction." OED, Washington, D.C.

Nicolai, S., and C. Triplehorn. 2003. "The Role of Education in Protecting Children in Conflict." HNP Network Series 42. London: ODI.

Pigozzi, M. 2000. "Education in Emergencies and for Reconstruction." Programme Division Working Paper. UNICEF, New York.

Sinclair, M. 2003. "Planning Education in and After Emergencies." Fundamentals of Educational Planning Series 73. Paris: UNESCO-IIEP.

Smith, A., and T. Vaux. 2003. "Education, Conflict and International Development." DFID Issues Paper, UK Department for International Development, London, February.

Sommers, M. 2002. "Children, Education and War: Reaching EFA [Education for All] Objectives in Countries Affected by Conflict." Human Development Network, Education Hub and Conflict Prevention and Reconstruction Unit (CPRU) Working Paper 1. World Bank, Washington, D.C.

UNESCO (United Nations Educational, Scientific and Cultural Organization). 2002a. "Guidelines for Education in Situations of Emergency and Crisis." Paris: UNESCO.

————. (United Nations Educational, Scientific and Cultural Organization). Division of Policies and Strategies of Education. 2002b. "Education in Emergencies: A Tool Kit for Starting and Managing Education in Emergencies." Paris: UNESCO.

UNHCR (United Nations High Commissioner for Refugees). "Education: Field Guidelines." Revised Version 2003. UNHCR: Geneva.

UNICEF (United Nations Children's Fund). "Education in Emergencies: A Planning Workshop Resource Kit" (forthcoming).

World Bank. 2003. *Breaking the Conflict Trap: Civil War and Development Policy.* Washington, D.C.: Oxford University Press/World Bank.

CHAPTER 2

Conflict, Poverty, and Education

Conflict has been conceptualized as "development in reverse" (World Bank 2003) and should be analyzed in the context of its impact on development. Reducing poverty and decreasing reliance on primary commodity exports, both of which require a functioning and effective education system, have been shown to be critical strategies for reducing the risk of conflict. Ethnic or religious dominance rather than diversity is also a powerful contributory factor in civil conflict; education has a key role in mediating or deepening ethnic, religious, and other identity-based conflicts. Civil war itself increases the likelihood of further outbreaks of conflict. Education that helps to build resilience to conflict is a critical strategy for reducing the risk of relapse into violent conflict.

CONFLICT AFFECTS COUNTRIES AT ALL LEVELS of economic development, but it disproportionately affects least developed countries or countries in economic stagnation. Conflicts vary widely in their nature, extent, duration, range of contributory factors, and the ways in which they impact education. Using the Uppsala dataset of Armed Conflicts 1946-2001[1], this study identified 52 countries or territories[2] that have been affected by war or intermediate conflict since 1990. These countries were then compared on the United Nations Development Programme's Human Development Index that combines a number of indicators of social and economic development into a single index and ranks countries accordingly.

Almost 60 percent of countries rated "low" on the Human Development Index have been involved in conflicts since 1990, in contrast to less than 25 percent of the 84 countries that have a "medium" rating. Long-term interest free loans are granted by the World Bank Group through the International Development Association (IDA) to countries that meet certain criteria, especially in terms of a gross national income per capita threshold (currently US$865). Countries that qualify for both IDA credit and International Bank for Reconstruction and Development (IBRD) loans are known as "IDA Blend" countries. The

World Bank Group rates two thirds (35) of 52 conflict countries "IDA" or "IDA Blend." Nine of these countries are currently covered by World Bank Transition Support Strategies (TSS). One third (17) are in the list of Low Income Countries Under Stress (LICUS), including six of the seven pilot LICUS countries. Forty percent (21) of these countries are Heavily Indebted Poor Countries (HIPC), although four (Liberia, Myanmar, Somalia, and Sudan) are rated "IDA Inactive" because of outstanding arrears, and a further eight had applied for HIPC assistance but had not reached "Decision Point" (at which eligibility for debt relief is determined) as of March 2003.

More than 50 countries have been involved in war or intermediate conflict since 1990.[3] The impact of conflict has been felt in every region, but Africa and Central and Eastern Europe have been particularly affected since 1990. More than half of the wars have been fought in these two regions, both of which include a high proportion of economies that have declined or stagnated in the past decade. Economic stagnation or decline preceded the outbreak of conflict in all the case study countries.

Factors Affecting Conflict Risk

Economic Factors. Reducing poverty is a critical strategy for reducing the likelihood of civil war. Poverty on its own is not a cause of violent conflict, since many poor countries are not seriously affected by civil war, and middle-income and developed countries are not immune. However, poverty is associated with an increased risk of civil war. Collier and Hoeffler (2000) cited in a recent World Bank analysis identify three economic factors that influence the likelihood of conflict:

- Low level of per capita income
- Low rates and/or stagnation in per capita income
- High dependence on primary commodity exports.

Collier and Hoeffler (2000) assert that doubling per capita income approximately halves the risk of civil war when controlled for other variables. Education is well established as a necessary but insufficient condition for economic development and poverty reduction.

Economic diversification is an important factor influencing the likelihood of civil war. High dependence on primary commodity exports increases the risk by as much as 33 percent (Collier and Hoeffler 2000). Where dependence on primary commodity exports is reduced to less than 10 percent of gross domestic product (GDP), the risk of conflict falls to 10 percent. Economic diversification requires the development of new and flexible skills and competences that require a functioning and efficient education system.

Identity-Based Factors. Ethnic and religious diversity are associated with a lower risk of civil war, except in cases of ethnic or religious domination or polarization. Societies in which the largest ethnic group constitutes between 45 percent and 90 percent of the population (termed "ethnic dominance") have a risk of violent rebellion that is about one third higher (Collier and Hoeffler 2000). Where this ethnic dominance does not exist, ethnic and religious diversity actually lower the risk of violent civil conflict. Education systems and schools, which are widely expected to play a role in mediating the relationship between ethnic and religious groups and so build "social capital," at the same time often stand accused of deepening conflict among ethnic, religious, and other social groups.

Civil War Factors. Civil war itself increases the risk of further conflict. Countries that have experienced a civil war in the preceding decade are almost twice as likely to experience rebellion, although this risk decreases at about one percentage point per year (Collier and Hoeffler 2000). If education is to have an impact on reducing the likelihood of conflict, the reconstruction and simultaneous reform of the system must begin at the earliest possible stage.

Educational Factors. Schools and education systems can create or exacerbate the conditions that contribute to conflict. Recently there has been a growing recognition of the role that schools and education systems can play in reproducing many of the factors that underlie much civil conflict.[4] Education systems and schools, which tend to reproduce the skills, values, attitudes, and social relations of dominant groups in society, are frequently a contributory factor in conflict. Inadequate education provision; racial, ethnic, or other forms of discrimination; distorted curricula; and frustrated expectations exacerbate existing social tensions or may themselves generate new sources of tension in societies.

In the case of Angola, for instance, that the education system substantially favored the *assimilados*[5] was an explicit complaint that recurred as a key area of conflict among the three major groups regarding power sharing in postindependent Angola. In Burundi, unequal education access on ethnic lines was a critical factor influencing the outbreak of war. Jackson (2000, p. 21) spells out the need for equal access to education in postconflict Burundi, noting that "... if access to education remains unequal for Hutu, Tutsi, and Twa, and if glaring disparities in education provision between different provinces persist, the exclusion that is at the root of Burundi's conflict will remain and any peace agreement will be short-lived." The disparity at the tertiary level was a particular source of resentment, with Tutsi students, a minority in the population, constituting a majority of university students.

In Kosovo, access to education was explicitly based on ethnic identity: Kosovar Albanian children were forced to leave the Kosovo public schools in the early 1990s, and the "parallel system" established in its place came to be seen as a symbol of the Kosovar Albanian struggle against Serb rule. In Timor Leste, despite relatively high enrollment rates, school achievement was significantly lower for Timorese than in the rest of Indonesia: 80 percent of the 16–18 year old age group had completed three years of education in 1998, compared with nearly 100 percent in Indonesia. More significant were substantial gaps between rich and poor, urban and rural, and male and female.

Curriculum impacts and is impacted by conflict. Three key themes run through the literature and experience on the relationship between curriculum and conflict:

- Languages and medium of instruction
- Standardized curricula that plural societies maintain, a "fictive image of cultural homogeneity" (Tawil 2003, p. 11)
- Perceptions of bias or exclusion in the curriculum

Sri Lanka offers the most vivid example of curriculum changes serving as an explicit issue in conflict, where a shift in medium of instruction to the national languages in the 1950s and 1960s "... resulted in fewer opportunities for interaction between Sinhalese and Tamil children and youth. Divided by language and ethnicity they increasingly lost the ability to communicate with each other, leading to alienation and mutual suspicion" (Wickrema and Colenso 2003, p. 5). In the 1970s the extremely limited access to tertiary education based on strict quotas led to a reduction in the number of Tamil students gaining admission to universities, with adverse consequences: "These developments, together with the depressed economic conditions and high unemployment of the middle 1970s, provided fertile grounds for the birth of youthful militant Tamil separatist groups...." (World Bank 1998, p. 128). In Kosovo, the medium of instruction, as well as imposition of the Serbian curriculum from Belgrade, were critical factors in the development of the parallel system.

It is not only the official curriculum that plays a significant role in exacerbating conflict. The widely differing quality of school facilities and funding in Cambodia, Kosovo, Sierra Leone, and Sri Lanka, for example, communicates clear messages about ethnic, religious, regional, or rural-urban biases that can generate as much resentment as explicit curriculum distortion. Years of conflict frequently result in school buildings being decorated with graphic depictions of the symbols of war; schools from Kosovo to Iraq, from Afghanistan to Liberia, frequently display murals of tanks, AK-47 assault rifles, or nationalist symbols. Most schools teaching through the medium of Albanian in Kosovo today have small shrines with pictures of staff, students, or community members who lost their lives in the struggle against Serb rule. Textbooks, the most influential artifact of the curriculum process, can also carry implicit messages as well as explicit biases in the form of messages about violence as a way of resolving issues or of glorification of the symbols of violence and domination. In Iraq, textbooks were heavily targeted for burning in the chaotic weeks that followed the collapse of the Saddam regime, partly because every textbook contained pictures of Saddam Hussein.

However, education and schooling also play a key role in several of the factors that build resilience to conflict in societies. The World Bank's Conflict Analysis Framework (CAF) lists "high youth unemployment" among its nine conflict risk indicators and includes "social and ethnic relations" as the first of six categories in the framework. Education systems and institutions have a critical impact on youth employment and on social and ethnic relations.

Characteristics of Resilience to Conflict

The CAF also identifies four characteristics of a society that is resilient to violent conflict:

- Political and social institutions that are inclusive, equitable, and accountable
- Economic, social, and ethnic diversity rather than polarization and dominance
- Growth and development that provide equitable benefits across society
- A culture of dialogue rather than violence

Education is a key social institution that is impacted by and can influence each of these characteristics. Just as education has the potential to be a contributory factor in violent conflict, it also has the potential to instill new values, attitudes, skills, and behaviors as well as help promote new social relations that will build resilience to conflict. Education can help to reduce economic, social, and ethnic polarization, promote equitable growth and development, and build a culture of dialogue rather than violence. Ensuring that schooling and education systems play a constructive role requires a closer understanding of the way in which conflict impacts education systems.

Endnotes

1. Uppsala Conflict Data Project is a collaborative project between Uppsala University and the International Peace Research Institute, Oslo.
2. This list includes Kosovo and Timor Leste. Timor Leste did not exist as a separate country at the time the dataset was last updated, and Kosovo remains a Province of Serbia, although still under special protection of the United Nations.
3. The Uppsala dataset defines "war" as a violent conflict with at least 1,000 battle-related deaths in one year, and "intermediate conflict" as a conflict with more than 100 battle-related deaths over the entire conflict and at least 25 battle-related deaths per year.
4. See, for example, Smith and Vaux (2003).
5. This refers to persons who had developed close relationships with the authorities and so been "assimilated" into the culture of the colonial power.

References

Collier, P., and Anke Hoeffler. 2000. "Greed and Grievance in Civil War." World Bank Policy Research Working Paper 2355, Washington, D.C.

Smith, A., and T. Vaux. 2003. "Education, Conflict and International Development." DFID Issues Paper, UK Department for International Development, London, February.

Tawil, S., and A. Harley, eds. 2004. *Education, Conflict and Social Cohesion.* Geneva: UNESCO International Bureau of Education.

Wickrema, A., and P. Colenso. 2003. "Respect for Diversity in Education Publication–The Sri Lankan Experience." Unpublished paper presented at the World Bank Colloquium on Education and Social Cohesion, Washington, D.C., March 23–25.

World Bank 1998. *Sri Lanka Social Services: A Review of Recent Trends and Issues.* Washington, D.C.: World Bank.

———. 2003. *Breaking the Conflict Trap: Civil War and Development Policy.* Washington, D.C.: Oxford University Press/World Bank.

CHAPTER 3

The Impact of Conflict
on Education

Conflict has a devastating impact on education, both in terms of the suffering and psychological impact on the pupils, teachers, and communities, and in the degradation of the education system and its infrastructure. Yet research also demonstrates that schools and education systems are surprisingly resilient, and the disruption caused by conflict offers opportunities as well as challenges for social reconstruction.

SCHOOLS RARELY ESCAPE THE RAVAGES of violent conflict. The first and most obvious impact of conflict on education is the loss of life and physical and psychological trauma experienced by teachers and students, parents, siblings, and community members either directly as targets of war or indirectly as victims in the crossfire. The havoc on the lives of students and teachers lasts long after violent conflict ends as a result of the detritus of war–landmines and unexploded ordinance and the proliferation of readily available arms and ammunition. Some schools in Cambodia and Angola will not be usable for decades because they are in areas where the costs of demining are prohibitive, and whole villages simply have been flagged as no-go areas.

Teaching forces are often severely debilitated by conflict. In Rwanda, more than two-thirds of the teachers in primary and secondary schools were either killed or fled; in Cambodia the carnage was even greater, leaving the system with almost no trained or experienced teachers. In Timor Leste, the impact on teacher numbers of that relatively short conflict was uneven. In primary schools, 80 percent of the teachers were Timorese and remained; however, almost all secondary school teachers were Indonesian, and their failure to return left Timor Leste with almost no trained or qualified personnel for its secondary system and no access to tertiary education.

However, except in cases of genocide or extremely low initial enrollment rates, the impact on the teaching force is often more qualitative
than quantitative. The challenge for most countries in postconflict
reconstruction is not recruitment of new teachers but improving the
quality of the teaching force in terms of qualifications, experience, and
competence. Pupil-to-teacher ratios in most of the countries studied
were actually lower in the year following the conflict than in the year
prior to it. In Kosovo, the withdrawal of Albanian children from
public schools and the steady migration of Serb families from Kosovo
after 1989 left many public schools with very low enrollments, but
they were still staffed on a formula basis that resulted in extremely low
pupil-to-teacher ratios in many schools. Among the Kosovar Albanian
schools in the parallel system similar staffing norms, combined with a
reluctance of officials to dismiss teachers during the liberation struggle,
also resulted in low pupil-to-staff ratios by the end of the conflict.
Lebanon saw pupil-to-teacher ratios climb slightly in the early years of
conflict from 23:1 before the war to 32:1 in 1979, but sliding rapidly
to 15:1 in 1989, barely three years after the conflict. Afghanistan,
however, faces an enormous challenge. The extended period of conflict
and extremely low enrollment rates, exacerbated during the latter
years of Taliban rule, mean that the output of the secondary system
cannot keep pace with the demand for primary teachers and cannot
grow at a fast enough pace until the cohorts of pupils from the
expanded primary schooling system reach secondary school age to
train as teachers.

The demand for teaching positions and teachers tends to grow
rapidly during early postconflict reconstruction as returnees, demobilized combatants, and unemployed turn to a very constricted labor
market. Rationalization[1] and redistribution rather than large-scale
recruitment are the most common teacher management problems
facing new or interim education authorities. Kosovo provides a recent
example of this. Some 2,000 "ghost" teachers were eliminated from
the payroll in 2000 to reduce the pupil-to-teacher ratios to more
sustainable levels. A recent survey in Sierra Leone identified almost
4,000 teachers who were on the payroll but not actively teaching.
Postconflict rationalization also affected Timor Leste, where new
staffing ratios provided for substantially higher pupil-to-teacher ratios
at the primary level in the reconstructed system. However, considerable numbers of teachers who did not meet minimum qualifications
continue to teach as "volunteer teachers," usually supported by
communities.

While teacher numbers may even grow and pupil-to-teacher ratios
decline during conflict and its immediate aftermath, the quality of the

teaching force frequently suffers. Teacher development is an early casualty of conflict, and the impact is long term. This includes both inservice training and initial teacher training. As a result, even where teacher numbers remain high or even grow, teacher qualification levels, often low to begin with, tend to drop significantly. By the end of the conflict, for example, only 50 percent of Lebanon's teachers were qualified, a pattern that can be found in most of the conflict-affected countries reported here. In addition, well qualified teachers may be induced by emerging employment opportunities to leave the profession and may be replaced by unqualified or underqualified persons.

Displacement, either within the country's borders or across borders, places enormous pressures on education systems and results in millions of learning days lost. Globally there are at least 50 million displaced persons, of which around half are cross-border refugees and the remainder are internally displaced (World Bank 2000). At least 12 countries have more than 200,000 of their own citizens taking refuge in neighboring countries and areas as a result of conflict, including five with over 400,000—Afghanistan, Angola, Burundi, Palestine, and Sudan (Table 3.1). Population shifts precipitated by conflict often are not easily reversed after conflict and may result in rapid urbanization with congestion of urban schools and depopulation of rural areas. Conflict has the effect of eroding the core values of societies. Children are orphaned, recruited, or separated from their parents; teachers and children are traumatized by violence; education systems and curricula

Table 3.1 Refugee Populations above 200,000 Located within Same Region as Country of Origin

Palestinian	4,044,500
Afghan	2,025,350
Sudanese	462,000
Burundi	421,000
Angolan	400,000
Sierra Leonean	389,000
Eritrean	355,800
DR Congolese	342,000
Croatian	314,700
Vietnamese	295,800
Burmese	258,750
Somali	247,700
Salvadorean	235,500
Bosnian	234,600

Source: Sommers 2002.

are politicized; and a culture of violence is reflected in school practices and even textbooks. The immediate symptoms are often quickly recognized in postconflict contexts in the form of blatant exclusion or curriculum distortions that are manifested in biased textbooks. However, the erosion of core values penetrates much more deeply and has a longer lasting impact than these peripheral symptoms. War transforms the roles of children and youth in ways that become extremely difficult to reverse. In a context where families and communities are often divided or dispersed by the upheaval of conflict, schools are seen as key institutions that will play the major role in rebuilding core values, in instilling new democratic principles, and in helping children recover lost childhood.

Destructive Effects of Conflict

Conflict is enormously destructive of educational infrastructure and buildings. Timor Leste, which experienced a short but intense spasm of violence following the independence referendum in 2000, is perhaps the most extreme example, with an estimated 95 percent of classrooms destroyed or seriously damaged in the conflict. Schools and classrooms are frequently targeted in civil conflict because they are seen to represent the state, but they also suffer damage from a range of other causes; as public buildings they are often commandeered as barracks, used for storage, looted, or occupied by displaced persons.

In many cases it is difficult to differentiate between damage resulting directly from violent conflict, and effects of years or decades of official neglect in the period prior to and during the conflict, as in Kosovo. In Iraq, the deterioration of the primary and secondary school infrastructure was largely a consequence of neglect. At the tertiary level this was compounded by extensive looting during the violent aftermath of the collapse of the Saddam regime. In Afghanistan the effect of decades of conflict was a failure to carry out the expansion of system capacity that neighboring countries undertook in the 1980s and 1990s. The backlog of physical capacity and trained teachers left the country with a legacy that will take decades to address. Whatever the cause, postconflict reconstruction almost invariably requires extensive capital investment to effect repairs and rehabilitation of buildings and physical infrastructure (Table 3.2).

Enrollment Rates.   Not surprisingly, conflict almost always involves a significant decline in enrollment rates during periods of intense conflict. Reliable enrollment data during conflict are very rare, but the

Table 3.2 Schools Requiring Repair or Reconstruction after Conflict (%)

Timor Leste	95
Iraq	85
Kosovo	65
Bosnia-Herzegovina	50
Mozambique	45

general pattern in the countries studied was that periods of intensified conflict saw precipitous declines in enrollment at all levels. However, there was also evidence of fairly rapid recovery in enrollment rates as intensity levels declined, even before peace agreements delivered consolidated stability. Figure 3.1 from Burundi shows a fairly typical pattern with rapid decline in enrollment rates following the crisis in 1993, followed by a fairly steady recovery. The period of conflict saw stagnation in enrollments during the conflicts in El Salvador and Guatemala, so that by 1989 both countries had only made limited progress on expanding primary enrollment, and secondary and post-secondary enrollments were well below the regional averages. Nicaragua, on the other hand, made significant progress in expanding primary access even during the years of the conflict, climbing from 58 percent Gross Enrollment Rates (GER) in the 1970s to 94 percent by 1989. This was partly a result of a determined campaign of the Sandanista government, and partly a result of significant international

Figure 3.1 Burundi: Gross Enrollment Rate, 1988–1999

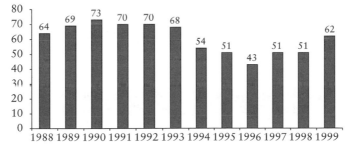

support from donors eager to support the populist program of the Sandanista government (Marques and Bannon 2003).

One impact of conflict on education systems that recurred frequently in this study was imbalance in the system among primary, secondary, and tertiary subsectors. While enrollment rates in primary schooling normally decline as a result of conflict, enrollment in secondary and tertiary levels tends to collapse more dramatically for a number of reasons.

- Students in secondary and tertiary institutions are more often closer to conscription age and are frequently among the early cohorts of recruits into military service.
- Students are often involved, especially at the tertiary level, as activists in the political struggles that precede conflict, and so universities and postsecondary colleges tend to be targeted more often.
- Secondary and tertiary institutions are more expensive to operate and maintain and are less likely to be able to subsist on community resources as official resources for education decline.

Capacity-Building.   It is the accumulated backlogs in human and institutional capacity that add most significantly to the burden of postconflict reconstruction. The damage to the physical infrastructure is one of the more easily rectified forms of conflict damage. More challenging is the deterioration in human and institutional capacity-building that is the lifeblood of any education system. Teacher training frequently collapses, learners drop out, management development and training and policy development break down, and resources are channeled to military expenditures and away from education, leaving schools without textbooks and learning materials, teachers unpaid, and schools unsupervised. In Timor Leste 20 percent of primary teachers, 80 percent of secondary school teachers, and almost all management officials were Indonesians trained outside of Timor Leste. They left when the conflict erupted and did not return. Almost all the countries studied experienced a serious depletion of management capacity, and in many cases equally serious loss of records and management information.

Data Collection and Integrity.   The instability that usually precedes conflict, in conjunction with the disruption created during conflict, have a very serious impact on education data for planning and policy. Even in countries where education data were systematically collected before the conflict, the decline or collapse of civil administration in all or part of the country often results in large gaps in policy and planning data, and even official distortions or willful destruction of official data. In Kosovo the parallel education system for Albanian Kosovars, which operated without official support for eight years of low-intensity conflict, experienced systematic destruction of records by Serb authorities during the intensified conflict and North Atlantic Treaty Organization (NATO) bombing campaign. This left the challenge of reconstruction with no reliable database on numbers of teachers, schools, and facilities. In countries such as Burundi, on the other hand, official statistics were published for every year even through the most serious phases of conflict, and the challenge for reconstruction is in determining the validity of the official data. In some cases officials went to exceptional lengths to protect official data and records. In Iraq, many officials took their official computers home and were able to help partially restore some information systems, although not enough to counteract the effect of the extensive looting and burning of headquarters and other official buildings.

System Management.   System management and development usually come to a standstill during conflict, as administration and supervision of learning are disrupted and policy development is suspended, distorted by competing political agendas, or fragmented. Education systems, often highly centralized prior to conflict, frequently experience fragmentation as the management systems, communication, and control are disrupted. Management and administrative structures wither or are prevented from operating; policy and curriculum development often grind to a halt, leaving, in the case of extended conflict, outdated policies, inappropriate and inadequate curricula, and neglected and deteriorating infrastructure. Sri Lanka offers an interesting exception to this general trend, as policy development and reform accelerated during the latter stages of conflict, and some reforms were even implemented in conflict-affected areas, although coverage and depth were lacking.

Gender Dynamics.   The relationship between gender and conflict is complex and intricate. While its manifestation varies considerably with the context, the gender dynamic is a critical dimension of the interaction between education and conflict. During conflicts, girls frequently have to take on unconventional roles in the family as their mothers cope with survival needs of their families or have to serve as heads of households. For girls, getting to and from school becomes even more of a personal safety hazard during periods of conflict and during the instability of early reconstruction.

- It is clear from the literature and data that, in most cases, girls are at a significant disadvantage in conflict-affected countries in terms of access to primary school, and this disadvantage is usually much higher at the secondary and higher levels. These inequities usually reflect the development conditions and gender relations of the country prior to conflict and are frequently compounded by conflict. While a significant number of conflict-affected countries report high gender inequities in access at primary and especially postprimary levels, these inequities can be found in many countries not affected by conflict. In Angola, gender inequities favored men in both urban and rural areas. The percentage of women who did not complete grade four in urban areas was four times higher than that for men (UNICEF 1996). The gender gap in access to education was consistently in favor of boys throughout the war period in Angola, although it narrowed slightly from around 13 percent in 1991 to as low as 7 percent in 1997, largely as a result of a more rapid decline in boys' enrollment rather than any net gains by girls. In 1998, the rapid return to school with the hope of peace, opened the gap again as boys flooded back to school at a faster rate than girls, only to revert to the previous pattern when the peace initiative collapsed at the end of 1998. Postconflict Angola continues to struggle with gender inequity. The government has introduced adult education schools and a positive discrimination quota to improve access among female students. The number of female professionals in areas previously dominated by men has increased (SADC 1999). However, a substantial population of Angolan women remains illiterate, uneducated, and suffering the consequences of war.

- The country studies illustrate a number of examples where the primary enrollment gender gap actually declines during conflict, usually as more boys are drawn into conflict. The data for Angola, Kosovo, and Lebanon provide some illustrations of this trend. The case of Burundi shows that the closing of the gender gap is a consequence not of increased access of girls but of greater decline in the enrollment of boys. It is worth noting that as the declining level of conflict permits more children to return to school, the gender gap widens again to near preconflict levels (Figure 3.2).

Quality.   The most profound and lasting impact of conflict on primary education, however, is on quality rather than access. Quality tends to deteriorate as qualified teachers disperse, as learning materials and supplies become less available, and as the length of the school day is reduced to accommodate two or more shifts per day. The legacy

Figure 3.2 Burundi: Net Enrollment Rate, 1990-2000

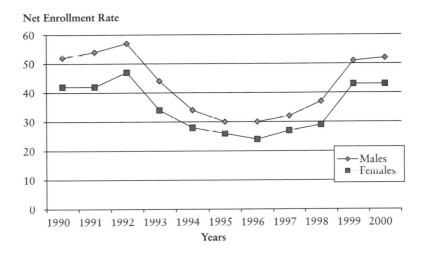

of dropout and repetition, disrupted attendance, and overage students greatly outlasts the frequently quite rapid recovery of enrollment rates. Outdated and inappropriate curricula, inadequately prepared teachers, collapsed teacher training, support and supervision services, and poor alignment of the system to the development needs of the country continue to undermine the quality of learning for many years after the problems of access have been addressed.

Surprising Resilience of Educational Systems

A striking feature of education during conflict is that it almost never comes to a complete standstill for an extended period. As public systems collapse under the effects of conflict, schooling continues to be supported by communities that see the benefits of education in helping to restore a sense of normalcy in the midst of chaos and providing a protective environment and sense of continuity for young people. The most dramatic exception to this was Cambodia, where schooling was brought to a complete standstill and teachers were systematically killed. In some countries, rebel movements, recognizing the potential propaganda value of schooling, support spontaneous or rebel schools (El Salvador, Guatemala, and Sri Lanka); in almost all cases communities struggle to continue provision of schooling even under the most difficult conditions, using alternative accommodation and flexible or multiple shifts. In areas not directly affected by conflict, schooling generally continues, albeit with reduced public support and a consequent deterioration in quality; Bosnia-Herzegovina, Kosovo, and Sierra Leone introduced shorter school days during the conflict to accommodate double and triple sessions. Kosovar refugees arriving in Albania and Macedonia quickly set up temporary schools to ensure continuity during the intensified conflict and NATO bombing in early 1999. For internally displaced families in Kosovo, and for most who remained in their home towns, schooling came to a complete standstill from only April to June 1999.

This resilience may be reflected in continued schooling during conflict, but equity, access, and quality usually deteriorate. Poorer families and child-headed households are often unable to meet the rising private costs of schooling. Boys and sometimes girls are withdrawn for military or other labor, or increased poverty or child-care responsibilities tend to exacerbate or distort existing gender and other inequities. Conflict-affected areas fall behind parts of the country not directly affected by conflict, and rural-urban inequities are exacerbated. In most cases, even where schooling is paralyzed by periods of intense conflict, enrollment in school recovers rapidly following conflict. In the short term, education access suffers seriously as a result of conflict leaving a lasting impact and developmental lag. However, primary schooling was quickly restored to preconflict levels in most of the countries studied. Figure 3.3 charts the GER in study countries in the year prior to the outbreak of conflict and the year following the cessation of hostilities, or the present year for countries emerging from conflict.

Figure 3.3   Gross Enrollment Rates and Conflict

Gross Enrollment Rate

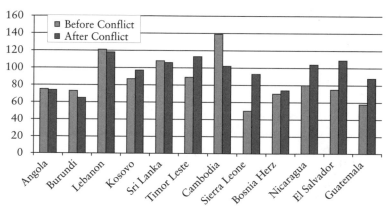

While official data on enrollment in such circumstances must be treated with caution, the general trend from these figures is upward, with higher primary enrollment rates in the year following conflict than in the year before. Sierra Leone, although seriously affected by the conflict, was able to report a very substantial primary enrollment growth (260 percent over 10 years previously) within two years of the end of conflict (Musker 2003), again giving evidence of the relative resilience of the primary sector and also the international priority placed on restoring primary schooling.[2] Angola and Burundi, countries that were still experiencing residual conflict despite ongoing peace talks, both show a slight decline. Where GERs in the year before conflict exceed 100 percent (Cambodia, Lebanon, and Sri Lanka), there is movement downward toward 100 percent as the overage children in the primary schools tend to be eliminated during periods of conflict.[3]

This crude measure does not take account of the growth that would have taken place had the system not been involved in conflict. Sommers (2002) presents one attempt to calculate lost student years as a result of conflict using as a basis a projection of preconflict enrollment trends. He offers estimates for Burundi, Democratic Republic of Congo, Rwanda, Sierra Leone, and Yugoslavia. While this type of counterfactual estimate must be viewed with considerable caution, these data offer crude evidence with respect to three countries (Burundi, Democratic Republic of Congo, and Federal Republic of Yugoslavia) of the substantial student years lost after the conflict erupted. In each case more student years were lost for boys than for girls. However, for Rwanda and Sierra Leone, the same methodology suggests substantial student years were gained after the conflict; the strongest trend was for Rwanda. Figure 3.4 is based on a more systematic study of enrollment patterns through the conflict years in Rwanda. It certainly suggests that Rwanda has been able to get back on its preconflict development track and now has a trajectory steeper than prior to the genocide. However, the total number of student years lost still has not been recovered.

The secondary and tertiary systems display less consistent patterns of resilience, although they frequently suffer equal or greater damage during conflict, and the GERs begin from a much lower base. In Timor Leste, where primary enrollment rates were restored very rapidly to preconflict levels, there was far less progress in enrollment rates at secondary and tertiary level. A comparison of enrollment by single age of the population in Timor Leste shows a significant increase between the 1998 and 2001 academic years for each age group below 15 years, and a steady decline for ages above 16 years (ET Ed and Poverty 2002 Figure 3.5). This was partly because rates were already low, and many

Figure 3.4 Enrollment Trends in Rwanda, 1970–2001

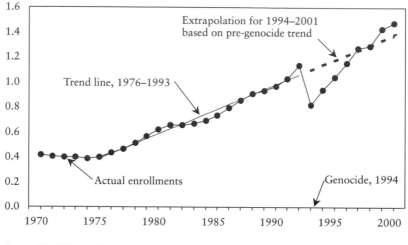

Source: World Bank 2003.

Figure 3.5 Enrollment Trends in Timor Leste, 1976–2002

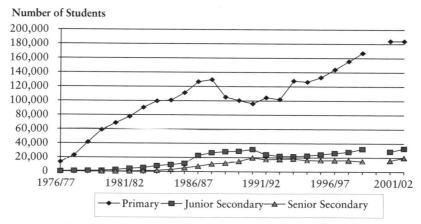

Source: World Bank 2001.

of the higher level students were children of Indonesian parents who left at independence.

However, it also reflects the greater resources that higher levels of education require. While primary schooling can be quickly initiated by communities even before there is a coherent support system, secondary schooling and tertiary education require greater investment of resources and institutional capacity. Secondary and tertiary education have a systemic lag as they can only expand at the rate of output of the primary system and therefore cannot demonstrate the kind of explosive expansion experienced in postwar Afghanistan primary schooling until those cohorts reach the secondary school age. In Bosnia-Herzegovina and Kosovo, secondary enrollment rates, which have barely recovered their prewar levels, remain among the lowest in the region.

The situation in the other countries studied varies significantly, with greater growth in immediate postconflict enrollment rates in those countries that experienced extended conflict. Slow progress in the expansion of secondary and tertiary education tends to generate a backlog of frustrated and unemployed youth ripe for recruitment into violence or crime. In addition to its impact on security and social stability, this situation hampers economic development and, in the longer term, weakens the entire educational system. Two clear implications emerge from this: the importance of focus on sector-wide reconstruction, and the need to attend to the learning needs of youth who lost out on educational opportunities as a result of conflict and who run the risk of becoming a "lost generation" for the education system and the wider society.

Postconflict Reconstruction Conundrum

For education reform and transformation, the postconflict reconstruction environment is the best of times and the worst of times, both an opportunity and a constraint. It is the best of times because the postconflict reconstruction environment offers significant opportunities for policy reform and system change:

- As old political regimes are challenged or replaced, more political space opens up.
- Communities and the public at large have high expectations for change and renewal in education.
- The resistance of established bureaucracies to change is often weakened.

- New and more flexible resources become available.

However, these same opportunities for reform contain their own constraints:

- Contested or weak political authorities are not well positioned to provide the political vision and leadership required for reform.
- Civil society is often in disarray as a result of conflict, or if organized, more experienced in oppositional politics than policy development.
- The lack of an effective administration makes implementing reforms extremely difficult.
- The unpredictability of financial flows makes long-term planning for reform particularly challenging.

Legacy of Conflict. Conflict adds a substantial additional burden to the daunting challenges of education development and reform. The legacy of conflict imposes significant additional burdens on education reform. Already mentioned are the accumulated backlogs in physical infrastructure, supplies and equipment, policy and system development, teacher development and training, and overage children. There are additional groups of learners with special needs (child soldiers and other war-affected youth, orphans, and disabled children). Additional pressures are exerted on the curriculum to simultaneously modernize, streamline, and include additional conflict-related content, such as landmine awareness, health and safety messages, psychosocial support, conflict management skills, and tolerance and respect for diversity.

Moreover, postconflict education systems also confront most of the challenges faced by systems in countries affected by poverty, economic crisis, mismanagement, or neglect. Much of postconflict reconstruction in education involves familiar development activities, the "usual business," of developing and reforming the education system—yet it is usual business in very unusual circumstances. Further, the "unusual business" arising from the conflict legacy can only be undertaken as part of an education development and reform program that places countries back onto a more conventional development path linked to the familiar development mechanisms such as Poverty Reduction Strategy Papers (PRSP), HIPC, sector-wide planning, and EFA.

Not business as usual. The added demands created by conflict, the scale of the reconstruction challenge, the urgency to avoid relapse into violence, and the extremely difficult operating conditions call for strategies and programs that address both the usual development challenges and the additional problems created by conflict in new and innovative ways. Even though many of the development tasks are familiar, education programming in postconflict societies cannot be "business as usual." Education has a critical role to play in the wider reconstruction of the society, from building peace and social cohesion to facilitating economic recovery and getting the country onto an accelerated development path. This places very considerable expectations on educational systems at a time when they are themselves seriously debilitated by the effects of conflict. The challenges facing educational systems in such contexts are enormous, and the potential for failure to deliver on these expectations is high. Yet there are examples of promising directions and lessons learned from the experiences gained in a wide range of different conflict and postconflict environments.

Endnotes

1. When used by education managers this term usually means a reallocation of teachers to teaching positions to achieve a more efficient deployment of the teacher corps. More often than not it involves reduction in the number of teachers employed in the system, leading to a more affordable pupil-to-teacher ratio. In many cases it also involves identifying and eliminating names of persons on the payroll who may no longer be at their posts or who may not even exist–the so-called "ghost teachers."
2. It is important to note that enrollment declined significantly in the years immediately prior to and during the war and that the dramatic recovery in enrollment in 2001-02 was largely a result of the abolition of fees.
3. Gross enrollment rates can exceed 100 percent where large numbers of repeaters and overage children remain in school. This phenomenon tends to decline during conflict as these children are usually the first to drop out. In the case of these countries the GER decline also may reflect more realistic enrollment data.

References

Marquez, J., and I. Bannon. 2003. "Central America: Education Reform in a Post-Conflict Setting, Opportunities and Challenges." CPR Working Paper 4. World Bank Social Development Department, Washington, D.C.

Musker, P. 2002. "Education and Post-Conflict Reconstruction–Lessons from Experience: Case Study: Sierra Leone." Unpublished research report sub-

mitted to the Human Development Network Education Center, World
Bank, Washington, D.C.

SADC. 1999. Gender Equality in Education. Available: http://www.sardc.net/
widsaa/sgm/1999/sgm_ch7.html.

Sommers, M. 2002. "Children, Education and War: Reaching Education For
All (EFA) Objectives in Countries Affected by Conflict." CPR Working
Paper 1. World Bank Social Development Department, Washington, D.C.

UNICEF (United Nations Children's Fund). 1996. ANGOLA Multiple Indica-
tor Cluster Survey (MICS), New York: UNICEF. Processed.

World Bank. 2000. *World Development* Report 1999-2000. Washington,
D.C.: World Bank.

———. 2001. "Education Finance in East Timor: Transition Priorities and
Long Term Options." World Bank, Washington, D.C. Processed.

———. 2003. "Education in Rwanda: Rebalancing Resources to Accelerate
Post-conflict Development and Poverty Reduction." World Bank Africa
Human Development Department (AFTH3) Report 26036-RW. Washing-
ton, D.C.

CHAPTER 4

Preliminary Lessons

This chapter offers an overview of some of the preliminary lessons derived from the study, illustrated with examples of promising directions from individual countries.

MOST OF THE MAJOR CHALLENGES confronting postconflict reconstruction of education systems are the same as those confronting any effort at system reform. The World Bank recently undertook a review of developing countries to assess the extent to which they are "on track" for achieving the Millennium Development Goals (MDG) and Education for All (EFA) goals of universal primary completion and gender equity in primary and secondary education by 2015. The analysis covered a range of indicators including primary enrollment and completion and identified 89 countries that were rated "not on track" or "seriously off-track" to achieve Universal Primary Completion (UPC) by 2015. One quarter of the 60 countries rated "not on track" are among the 52 conflict-affected countries identified for this study, as are over one third of 29 seriously off-track countries. Conflict clearly constitutes a significant obstacle to achieving the EFA and MDG targets. Yet it is also true that at least 13 conflict-affected countries are "on track" to achieve universal primary completion, including Colombia, El Salvador, Kosovo, and Sri Lanka. Conflict was only one of several factors that contributed to the poor performance in achievement of international goals.

Key Factors

A set of case studies of successful countries identified four key factors that facilitate rapid expansion of primary education to achieve the MDG targets, and they are as relevant in postconflict environments as in others. However, the additional constraints arising from conflict make addressing these factors even more challenging. The four factors were as follows:

- Sound policies and committed leadership at the country level, supported by appropriate expenditure frameworks, effective budget execution, and good governance
- Adequate operational capacity at all levels, including capacity of communities to participate effectively, and the right incentives, so that countries can translate sound policies and strong leadership into effective action
- Financial resources to scale up programs that work and measures to ensure that these reach the service delivery level
- Relentless focus on results and accountability for learning and outcomes, so that policies and programs are built on the bases of empirical evidence of problems and solutions that work.

These four factors still provide a framework for approaching the reconstruction of education after conflict, with the clear recognition that the starting points may be considerably further from the targets, the conditions make progress even more challenging, and the legacy of conflict adds an additional set of factors that must be addressed if the system is to recover.

Key Principles

Given the wide ranging nature of contexts that are covered by the term "postconflict" and the radically different starting points of many countries, it is useful to start from a set of key principles. The most systematic set of principles are those published by Sinclair (2003), which are clustered around issues of access, resources, activities/curriculum, coordination, and capacity-building. Box 4.1 provides a summary of Sinclair's framework.

The findings of this study suggest four additional principles that relate more specifically to postconflict reconstruction. These principles in many ways complement or supplement those articulated by Sinclair.

- Education is a development activity. While education and schooling may be an important "fourth pillar" of humanitarian assistance and critical for child and social protection, it is also from the beginning a development activity and should be oriented toward social, economic, and political development, and the longer term interests of the learners and the society.

Box 4.1 Sinclair's Principles of Emergency Education

Access
- The right of access to education, recreation, and related activities must be ensured, even in crisis situations.
- Rapid access to education, recreation, and related activities should be followed by steady improvement in quality and coverage, including access to all levels of education and recognition of studies.
- Education programs should be gender-sensitive, accessible to, and inclusive of all groups.
- Education should serve as a tool for child protection and harm prevention.

Resources
- Education programs should use a community-based participatory approach, with emphasis on capacity-building.
- Education programs should include a major component of training for teachers and youth/adult educators and provide incentives to avoid teacher turnover.
- Crisis and recovery programs should develop and document locally appropriate targets for resource standards, adequate to meet their educational and psychosocial objectives.

Activities/Curriculum
- All crisis-affected children and young people should have access to education, recreation, and related activities, helping meet their psychosocial needs in the short- and longer-term.
- Curriculum policy should support the long-term development of individual students and of society and, for refugee populations, should be supportive of a durable solution, normally repatriation.
- Education programs should be enriched to include skills for education for health, safety, and environmental awareness.
- Education programs should be enriched to include life skills for education for peace/conflict resolution, tolerance, human rights, and citizenship.
- Vocational training programs should be linked to opportunities for workplace practices of the skills being learned.

Coordination and Capacity-building
- Governments and assistance agencies should promote coordination among all agencies and stakeholders.
- External assistance programs should include capacity-building to promote transparent, accountable, and inclusive system management by local actors.

Source: Sinclair 2003.

- Education reconstruction begins at the earliest stages of a crisis. It is undertaken concurrently with humanitarian relief, assuming an increasing share of activities as the polity, civil society, administrative capacity, and access to resources develop. Education reconstruction has no sharp distinction between a humanitarian phase and a reconstruction phase.

- Postconflict education reconstruction is centrally concerned with conflict prevention to ensure that education does not contribute to the likelihood of relapse into violence and actively builds social cohesion to help prevent it. The lessons from postconflict education reconstruction should be applied in countries at risk of conflict and countries currently affected by conflict. One of the most significant contributions education can make is to help to reduce the risk of violence in at-risk countries.

- Postconflict reconstruction in education calls for a prioritized approach within a broad sector-wide framework. The focus on basic education that is strongly reflected in this study and in the literature is based on the recognition that primary education is the basis of the entire system and therefore warrants high priority. However, the clear evidence from this study is that without systematic focus on all subsectors (pre-primary, primary, secondary, and tertiary) and delivery modes (such as formal, nonformal, and distance), there is a danger that postconflict reconstruction will introduce or exacerbate imbalances in the system. Apart from the system and development logic underlying this argument is the simple fact that the recovery of the basic education system requires teachers who are produced in the secondary and tertiary subsectors.

Conflict Analysis

Education should be a central component of all conflict impact assessments or conflict risk analyses. The World Bank's Conflict Analysis Framework (CAF) is only one of at least 12 conflict analysis tools currently available. Most of these do not include analysis of the role of education in contributing to conflict or mitigating its effects. There is a growing need for supplementary tools that specifically focus on education issues, but these should be treated as components of wider conflict analyses rather than as stand-alone tools. The available tools vary from frameworks for extensive participatory studies to sets of concise checklists, and different types of analyses are clearly appropriate for different contexts. There is limited experience globally of integrating education into conflict assessments, and no specific examples of promising directions were identified. However, recognition of the importance of the issue was increasing in many of the countries studied.

While little consensus exists on the definition of "phases" of conflict and postconflict status, education reconstruction activities should begin concurrently with humanitarian assistance and be scaled up as political space, civil society support, administrative capacity, and resources permit. The issue of "phases" of conflict and postconflict reconstruction resurfaces regularly and is equally difficult to pin down for analytical purposes. As with definitions of conflict, there is a wide range of interpretations regarding whether and how different stages in a conflict are described. Every attempt elicits a list of exceptions and counter arguments. This stems from two causes. The first is the extremely wide range of contexts and conflicts that fall into the broad category of "conflict countries." The second is that many conflicts do not follow a simple progression from one "stage" to another; rather, they progress, regress, and/or stagnate. In many situations parts of a country may be in one "stage" while others are in a more advanced stage, or some areas may appear to be in two or more stages concurrently.

The World Bank's publication *"Post-Conflict Reconstruction: the Role of the World Bank"* proposes five stages as a framework for its activities based on the operational conditions in the country:

- Watching Brief in Conflict Countries
- Transitional Support Strategy
- Early Reconstruction Activities
- Postconflict Reconstruction
- Return to Normal Operations.

These stages are presented not as a framework for definition of conflict phases but to suggest a logical progression for Bank-supported activities. The focus thus shifts from classifying the country conditions to classifying the type of activities that the Bank should support. Rather than become enmeshed in further theoretical debate about the phases issue, this study suggests a simple framework designed to ensure a fit between objective conditions in the country and appropriate strategies and that this congruence is achieved within a developmental framework linked to longer-term reconstruction.

Operating Environment

An important factor influencing postconflict reconstruction activities is the operating environment for education. This study identifies four key indicators of such an environment:

- *Political authority*, which may range on a continuum from no legal or recognized political authority through interim (or competing) authorities and transitional or provisional governments to a functioning internationally recognized government.
- *Civil society*, which may range on a continuum from a situation where civil society is not consciously constituted through various situations involving limited civil society engagement or a strongly contested civil society to a stable and experienced civil society that can effectively engage in policy and system development.
- *Administrative capacity*, which may range from an apparent complete breakdown of education system administration even at the local level, through various levels of human, institutional, and operational capacity for administering education, to a fully functioning administration that reflects the balance of centralized and decentralized authority.
- *Resources for education*, which may range from a situation where public financing of education has completely collapsed through various combinations of public and private financing to a fully functioning financing system with a balance of public and private financing that ensures equity, quality, and access.

The conditions in each conflict-affected country will vary with respect to the above four dimensions. Accordingly, it is more helpful to review each country in terms of these variables to determine the nature and scale of reconstruction activities that are possible. They are represented in figure 4.1 as a series of continua, and each country may be placed at different points on each continuum.

This framework allows some flexibility to accommodate the complex range of circumstances that postconflict reconstruction encounters. The scale of reform activities that could be mounted in Iraq, for instance, where for the first year there was no indigenous civil authority, compares starkly with the kind of education reforms framed in El Salvador. In Iraq, the focus was at the level of resumption of learning and reform limited to purging the schools and the textbooks of the most extreme manifestations of the Baathist regime; in El Salvador the authorities implemented radical reforms regarding the governance

Figure 4.1 The Education Reconstruction Continuum

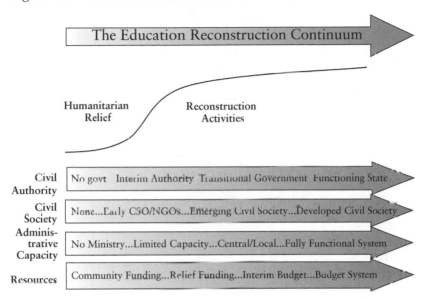

of the system. Nicaragua inherited a largely functioning administration that survived the political transition below top leadership levels, while in Kosovo the administrative infrastructure had almost totally disintegrated. In Kosovo this provided both the space for the introduction of fairly radical reforms in terms of community involvement in school governance and constraints on the ability of the interim authorities to implement them at the school level. Civil society had become a vibrant force for change in Guatemala and faced the challenge of transforming from the politics of opposition to the politics of policy development, while the repressive regimes in both Afghanistan and Iraq fostered civil society that had survived by remaining almost invisible. Unpredictable resource flows for both reconstruction and recurrent costs in Burundi contrast starkly with the situation in Timor Leste, where international agencies moved rapidly to establish trust funds to support reconstruction and provide some predictability for planning.

Sequencing Interventions

Appropriate sequencing of interventions is a key to successful postconflict reconstruction in education. The postconflict environment presents particular challenges in terms of priorities, since the range of issues demanding attention, the urgency for action, the complexity of the context, and the limited human, institutional, and financial resources often make prioritization extremely difficult. It is not uncommon in the heat of international pressure and community demand for textbook and curriculum development to get out of sequence, for peace education programs to run too far ahead of peacebuilding in communities or for decentralization initiatives to exceed the capacity of local authorities to implement them. The factor that makes analysis of sequencing so critical in postconflict situations is the urgency to take some action on almost all fronts: textbooks from the preconflict era may be unacceptable, guidance may be needed on managing community tensions in schools, local contributions to schooling may call for some mechanisms for community input to school management, schools may need to be built before there is agreement on construction and other standards. While there is no golden rule regarding the question of sequencing in postconflict reconstruction, this study suggests several starting points:

- First, focus on the basics to get the system functioning so that the return of children and youth to school can be seen as an early "peace dividend" that will help to shore up support for peace.
- Second, acknowledge the importance of symbolism in education and provide bold symbolic actions (such as purging textbooks) that signal that the reform of the system has started.
- Third, build recognition that reform of education is a long-term, incremental, and ongoing process that takes decades and that must be led from within the country as consensus develops on the wider development vision of that society.
- Fourth, focus from the beginning on building reform capacity, which includes supporting the participation of communities, local authorities, and other stakeholders in the educational reform dialogue. This can be initiated in early phases when there is a general anxiety about reform of the system, but not the political coherence, administrative capacity, civil society commitment, or financial and institutional resources required to implement systemic reform.

Leveraging Interim Arrangements and Transitional Mechanisms

The postconflict reconstruction environment often presents authorities, policymakers, and system managers with a wide range of "chicken-and-egg" problems in which policy in one issue depends on decisions made on a related issue. Teachers cannot be paid until they are appointed, and they cannot be appointed until there is agreement on a pay scale, and a pay scale cannot be determined until there is clarity on the number of teachers appointed at each level or the budget available for salaries. This is a manifestation of the sequencing problem, and successful responses have made use of interim arrangements with clear guidance on how long these arrangements will apply and what is being done to replace them with more permanent policies. In Kosovo, teachers were paid a stipend by the United Nations authorities until a more elaborate pay scale could be negotiated. In Iraq, all educational personnel were paid along with other public servants on a basic four-grade scale that was based on length of service, which resulted in some older support staff earning significantly more than the qualified educational staff in the schools.

Prioritizing within a System-wide Approach

While international support often prioritizes basic education and tertiary education, authorities are faced with the need to ensure balanced development of the system and to support the resumption and development of secondary education and technical and vocational and adult and nonformal subsectors. Large numbers of young people who may have missed out on basic education because of the conflict, or whose secondary education was disrupted, place additional pressures on the system. The need to restart teacher education, both inservice and preservice, presents additional challenges to postconflict education authorities and calls for creative solutions. Accelerated learning programs, "catchup classes," and summer schools and a transparent and clear system-wide development program have helped authorities respond to these pressures to a certain extent from Sierra Leone to Afghanistan. However, this study suggests that progress in the secondary, tertiary, and nonformal education almost always lags seriously behind basic education. El Salvador is one example of a reconstruction program that took a more sector-wide approach.

Building on Existing Initiatives

While postconflict environments present exciting opportunities and often considerable community demand for change, the reality is that new systems are not created from scratch but are built on the foundations of the previous system. Successful interventions recognize this and work with communities and officials to identify and build on the main strengths of the previous systems, incorporate beneficial practices and strategies that may have emerged during the conflict or among other groups, and identify a limited number of the most critical elements of the existing system to target for change. Attempting to change too many things at once often results in limited impact on the existing system, which usually demonstrates remarkable resilience and resurfaces even where it had apparently completely disintegrated. Kosovo provides an example of a context where the old "parallel system" [Albanian Kosovar] and the former Serbian provincial systems have demonstrated significant resistance to the wide-ranging reforms introduced by the UNMIK administration.

Demonstrating Early and Visible Impact

System reconstruction and development are slow. Much of the work that has to be done does not produce early outcomes with clear and visible impact. Successful initiatives have directed resources in early reconstruction to demonstrate quick and visible impact and to ensure that the credit for the achievement is shared with communities. Rehabilitation and repair programs, provision of learning materials, teaching supplies, equipment, furniture, and school grant programs can all help to build the confidence of communities in themselves and in the new authorities. Back-to-school campaigns such as those led by the United Nations Children's Fund (UNICEF) in Afghanistan, Kosovo, and Iraq provide examples. This confidence helps to sustain momentum and elicit support for the demanding challenge of simultaneous reform and reconstruction.

Encouraging Community Involvement

During most conflict situations the energy to sustain delivery of education shifts to communities and schools. In early reconstruction this energy provides critical momentum to get schools reopened and the system running. It is important that efforts to reconstruct the system do not undermine the level of community involvement and participation that is frequently engendered during conflict. In circumstances where new political authorities are enmeshed in difficult policy negotiations and where the administrative capacity of the system is weak, resources directed to schools and communities are critical to sustain the momentum of education provision. At the same time, mechanisms that deliver resources directly to schools and communities must be progressively integrated into the emerging administrative and monitoring system to avoid the development of parallel bureaucracies.

Early Initiation of Technical and Capacity-building Work

The emergence of policy vision and implementation capacity of the interim, transitional, provisional, or new authorities can be considerably accelerated by preliminary work on technical issues (such as collecting school and system data; conducting social assessments; exploring options and international experience on student assessment practices, and legislation options; or initiating management capacity-building The design of strategies, policies, and programs is a complex technical undertaking that should be based on thorough diagnosis of the state of the system and should clearly evaluate costs and options.

Some of the preparatory work need not even await an end to hostilities. In Angola, several initiatives to collect data on the system even during the years of conflict provided a base of statistics and some technical capacity than was an asset as the reconstruction began. While care must be taken to ensure that this work is undertaken in a transparent manner and is limited as far as possible to technical issues or development of options, it can prove to be an important resource for informing policy and developing implementation capacity as conditions permit. It is important that the technical work that is done is also part of a capacity-building strategy so that there is a commitment to and sense of ownership of the technical analyses and data. The window of opportunity to implement bold reforms is generally brief and is more likely to be used if based on solid technical analytical work.

Building Effective Partnerships

The postconflict situation sometimes creates conditions that make partnerships and interagency coordination very difficult at a time when it is most important. The sudden influx of resources that follows many high profile peace agreements can precipitate the "feeding frenzy" environment of intense competition among development partners and nongovernmental organizations for financial resources and visibility which official coordination mechanisms struggle to contain. National authorities may not yet be sufficiently consolidated to provide the strong and clear leadership and frameworks required

for effective coordination. During the transition from predominantly
humanitarian assistance to predominantly reconstruction activities,
there is often a need to restructure partnerships and reconfigure
coordination mechanisms to accommodate changes in resource flows
and political authority. The key to effective interagency coordination
in such contexts is movement as rapidly as possible to national leadership of the donor coordination process; in the interim, agreement
among agencies of "lead roles" (Kosovo) and on a single strategic
framework (Timor Leste) can help.

References

Sinclair, M. 2003. "Planning Education in and after Emergencies." Funda-
    mentals of Educational Planning No. 73. Paris: UNESCO IIEP.
World Bank. 1998. *Post-Conflict Reconstruction: The Role of the World
    Bank*. Washington, D.C.: World Bank.

CHAPTER 5

Promising Directions in System Reconstruction

This chapter provides some key lessons with examples of promising initiatives in the areas of joint assessment missions, initial policy and system reform, proactive political leadership, consolidation of central government authority, societal consensus-building, strengthening of school and community linkages, and coherent reconstruction policies.

Sector Assessment

Education sector assessment should be treated as an iterative process that builds on initial rapid appraisal and needs assessment exercises and widens gradually to include more issues, more informants, and more analysis. The postconflict environment often produces a flurry of needs assessments and rapid appraisals conducted by various actors and authorities. Coordination can help to make as many of these as collaborative as possible. Sector assessment in these contexts almost always involves a certain amount of duplication. Encouraging partners from different agencies to work closely with authorities and communities as early as possible can help to minimize this.

Joint assessment missions with key development partners and local specialists and officials provide valuable information and build relationships that are important for postconflict reconstruction, as the following examples illustrate:

- In Timor Leste, the World Bank coordinated a joint assessment mission in the first weeks after the conflict ended, developing important relationships and accumulating useful baseline information.
- In Afghanistan, an interagency Preliminary Needs Assessment (PNA) conducted in December 2001 and a later full Needs Assessment provided a basis of relationships and information for planning the humanitarian response and the initial reconstruction.

- In Sri Lanka, a Joint United Nations/World Bank/Asian Development Bank Needs Assessment of Education in the North East has been completed under the direction of a joint Government of Sri Lanka and Liberation Tigers of Tamil Eelam (LTTE) mechanism following agreements reached in the second round of peace talks.
- In Iraq, the Joint United Nations Development Programme/World Bank Needs Assessment, a multisectoral, multiagency assessment of needs undertaken in July and August of 2003, provided a basis for more effective coordination both among United Nations agencies and among the United Nations and other donors and agencies.

Challenges for Decentralization

Fundamental to successful outcomes are measures to ensure that consolidation of the system does not destroy the community participation and involvement in schooling and education. Reconstructing the education system in a postconflict situation presents particular challenges for the issue of decentralization. During conflict, previously highly centralized systems tend to fragment as the capacity of the central authorities is stretched and/or their legitimacy is questioned. Consequently, postconflict systems frequently have some of the features of decentralized systems, including high levels of community participation, stronger sense of ownership at local level, and greater responsiveness to local conditions. However, the system fragmentation is accompanied by declines in access, quality, and equity.

Early Policy and System Reform Preparation. This preparation, which includes technical work on Education Management Information Systems (EMIS), review of existing legislation and regulations, exploration of school and system governance options, diagnosis of the state of the system, and analysis of resource flows, can have a powerful impact when the momentum for reform builds and the civil authority increases its capacity.

- In Kosovo, early technical work on EMIS, decentralization, and legislation supported by the World Bank provided a good technical basis for system reconstruction as the capacity of the new civil authority developed.
- In Sierra Leone, the Rehabilitation of Basic Education Project (REBEP provided early support to decentralization and community involvement in school management.

Role of Political Leadership. The pace of system reconstruction is strongly influenced by the level of political leadership that can provide a clear vision and help to coordinate donors around it. A recent study of three Central American countries identifies this as the first of the eight key lessons (see Box 5.1).

- In El Salvador, continuity in the government allowed the ministry to provide clear leadership with strong support from other ministries and the head of state to implement a reform program in the early postconflict years.
- In Bosnia-Herzegovina, the lack of a shared political vision for system reform and the institutionalized fragmentation that was politically mandated by the Dayton Accords peace agreement presented significant challenges for successful decentralization.
- In Kosovo, the policy vision developed within the United Nations Mission in Kosovo (UNMIK) encountered resistance when the provisional government took power because it was perceived as having been imposed by international staff. However, the policy vision effectively cemented into place reforms that might have been difficult for the new national authorities to implement.
- In Angola, a 1992 World Bank report found that the decentralization policy to which the government was formally committed had not progressed because of lack of clear objectives and action plan.

Box 5.1 Summary of Key Lessons from Central America

- Develop a clear national vision on education reforms.
- Start the technical preparations of reforms as early as possible.
- Build a broad-based consensus on education reforms and on existing initiatives (EDUCO).
- Pay attention to the dialogue and consensus-building process.
- Move swiftly to earn trust and secure the support of critical stakeholders.
- Empower parents and involve them in their children's education to elicit broad support for reforms and to ensure their implementation.
- Modernize and decentralize the education ministry to avert bureaucratic derailing of the reform process.
- Focus on decentralization to schools, an agenda the education sector can control, as opposed to decentralization to local governments, a process that lies outside the control of the education sector.

Marques & Bannon 2003.

Consolidation of Authority.   In postconflict contexts, decentralization requires the consolidation of the central government authority.

- Successful decentralization in El Salvador was accompanied by
  the rationalization and modernization of the Education Ministry
  to help with the adjustment to its new role in a decentralized
  system.
- The National Recovery Strategy in Sierra Leone involved
  capacity-building for central and district education offices.
- The Management Empowerment Project in Kosovo provided
  three months of management training to orientate aspiring
  education officials to the new balance of centralized and
  decentralized capacity.
- In Bosnia-Herzegovina, where decentralization was driven by
  central ethnically-based political interests, problems were
  encountered when the pace of decentralization exceeded the
  capacity of the local management to implement it.

Societal Consensus-building.   Reform and restructuring of the system
in postconflict contexts require commitment to building social consensus for reform.

- A national campaign for education reform in El Salvador helped
  build consensus. In contrast, in Nicaragua the national consultation was not seen to be taken seriously by some government
  officials and was poorly supported.
- In Guatemala, the impact of the national commission was limited
  by the perception that many of the items on the agenda were
  driven by concerns of international actors.

Balanced Approach to Reform.   System reform requires a careful balance of building on the foundations of the previous system without reproducing the highly centralized control and inefficiencies typical of
the past.

- The 1995 New Education Policy for Sierra Leone, which
  contained progressive commitments to modernize the system and
  "build a free, just and peace-loving society," was not implemented. The policy did provide, however, a starting point for
  subsequent new legislation that includes provisions for
  decentralization of the system.
- Many of the system reforms in Sri Lanka, which were enacted
  during the conflict in areas unaffected by conflict, provided a
  legal basis for postconflict reforms.

- Part of the success of El Salvador's Education with Community Participation Program (EDUCO) is that it built on the successful community-controlled schooling that emerged during the conflict.
- Education reform in Kosovo encountered problems when it was not perceived as acknowledging the strengths of both the "parallel system" for Albanian children and the official system for Serb children.

Strengthening Schools and Community Linkages.   In early stages of postconflict reconstruction, while the authority of the government is being consolidated, the process of reform and decentralization is facilitated by programs that strengthen schools and their community linkages.

- World Bank-supported school grant programs in Bosnia-Herzegovina, Kosovo, and Sierra Leone are helping to promote community involvement in schools.
- The process of decentralization in El Salvador was facilitated at the local level by incentives to schools that chose to directly manage their funds. These incentives included bonuses for improvements in the quality of the school environment, teacher training allowances, and food voucher program in EDUCO schools.

Coherent Reconstruction Policy Mechanisms.   Effective donor coordination requires strong national leadership. In the absence of a strong political authority, clear and effective mechanisms are required to ensure coherence in reconstruction.

- Strong leadership from a confident political authority enabled El Salvador to ensure that donor support for education reconstruction was implemented in terms of a coherent national vision under the leadership of the government.
- The international practice of identifying "lead agencies" for education provides a helpful means of coordinating the activities of the international agencies during the humanitarian assistance phase, but it has not yet effectively brought coherence to interventions from bilateral and multilateral agencies or international nongovernmental organizations (NGO).
- The Lead Agency model in Kosovo took lead agency approach to a subsectoral level and assigned responsibility for key issues (such as curriculum development, teacher development, special

education, and technical and vocational education) to bilateral and multilateral agencies. These agencies were responsible for coordinating agencies and NGOs, mobilizing development resources, and implementing programs in their assigned areas. Although this enabled the United Nations interim authority UNMIK to remain relatively lean, it had some disadvantages in terms of limited coordination across subsectors and missed opportunities to build local capacity to facilitate the handover to local control.

Education Access

Experience has demonstrated that schools can reopen and teachers can resume work in circumstances where supervision and control, and even systems for appointment and payment of teachers, may not be operational. Targeting supplies and support to assist community initiatives, providing simple guidelines on key policy issues, and supporting the return to school with advocacy and communication campaigns are key strategies that promote success.

Community Initiative.   Back-to-school movements are usually driven at the grass roots level by communities themselves who often reopen schools and establish temporary learning spaces on their own initiative.

- In Kosovo, communities initiated a rapid resumption of schooling with significant support from international agencies and a back-to-school advocacy campaign that delivered supplies, textbooks, tents, and shelter materials.
- Through a combination of community action and international support in Timor Leste, 86 percent of classrooms were rehabilitated, 80 percent of furniture, and 50 percent of books were delivered to students within 18 months.
- In Sierra Leone, NGOs, the United Nations Mission in Sierra Leone (UNAMSIL), and government officials worked with communities to support the rapid resumption of learning.

Early resumption of schooling almost always builds on the previous system, using existing curricula, textbooks, facilities, and teachers.

- In Kosovo, UNMIK worked with international partners and local specialists to identify critical potential sources of conflict in the previous system (exclusion, biased curricula and textbooks, languages, and medium of instruction). UNMIK issued Interim

Arrangements for the Resumption of Schooling to provide guidance on how these issues could be addressed using existing teaching staff, institutional infrastructure, curricula, and textbooks.

Closing Gaps.   Expansion of access that prioritizes girls, poor communities, and rural areas can be an effective way of rapidly closing equity gaps. In Timor Leste, the rapid resumption and expansion of access significantly reduced equity gaps between boys and girls, poor and richer communities (figure 5.1), and urban and rural areas.

Quality Improvement

It is important to acknowledge that quality improvement is a process and requires an ongoing commitment. Postconflict situations sometimes induce an "access first, quality later" approach. The evidence from this study shows that the most profound and lasting impact of conflict on education was on quality rather than on access. The deterioration in quality, which represents one of the most significant challenges to reconstruction, should be a consideration from the outset.

Figure 5.1 Timor Leste Enrollment Poverty Gap, 2001

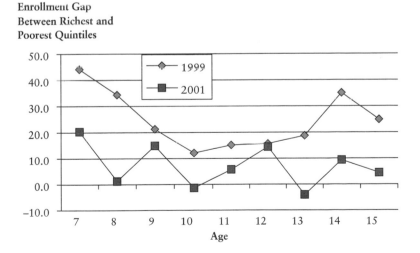

Enrollment Gap
Between Richest and
Poorest Quintiles

Quality is a concern of all communities, parents, teachers, and students. Strategies to tackle it are most successful when addressed as an ongoing process of quality improvement rather than striving to meet some external, official, or historically determined standard. Discussions about how to improve the quality of learning and of the learning environment are as critical in temporary learning spaces under trees or canvas as they are in established systems. An ongoing concern for quality in terms of inputs, processes, and outcomes is critical to ensuring that the reconstruction of the system does not simply reproduce the limitations of previous systems or sacrifice learning opportunities for externally imposed access targets.

Tradeoff Decisions. There are tradeoffs between investment in expansion of access and improvement of quality, and these are even more stark in the postconflict context. Clear tradeoff decisions have to be made between investing in preservice and inservice teacher education, for instance, or focusing on curriculum content, methods, or frameworks. The postconflict environment is one in which the issue of priorities becomes even more pressing than in other development contexts, not simply because of the constraints on resources but also because of key decisions around sequencing. Time becomes as critical a resource as money or human capital and adds new dimensions to the calculations related to prioritization.

Simplistic formulae such as "access first, quality later" become even less helpful in such contexts. Treating quality improvement as a key ongoing concern helps to provide a framework for discussions around priorities and sequencing. Such a concern for quality improvement as a frame of reference was a key factor in most of the promising directions and lessons learned that are described here and constitutes an important theme for effective interventions.

Community Involvement. Involving communities, parents, and teachers in discussions about quality improvement has strong returns in terms of recognizing quality improvement as a process.

- In Cambodia, school grants to schools and school clusters allocated as part of the Education Quality Improvement Project (EQIP) project helped engage parents with teachers and school authorities in strategies to improve the quality of the learning environment.
- In Bosnia-Herzegovina, school improvement grants to schools are awarded on the basis of school improvement plans that address issues of quality improvement.

Monitoring System Quality. Early technical work on standards and assessment can build a basis for improving the capacity of systems to monitor learning outcomes as a key mechanism for monitoring system quality.

- In both Kosovo and Bosnia-Herzegovina, initial work on establishing bodies for determining standards and assessment have helped focus attention of officials on the need for improved measurement of learning outcomes.

Qualified Teachers

Teachers are the most critical resource in education reconstruction. Conflict usually has profound and negative impact on a country's teacher corps. Frequently dispersed, sometimes killed, and often unpaid or underpaid, teacher supply presents a complex array of problems for reconstruction. Reconstruction usually begins with a cohort of existing teachers inherited from both previous system and the spontaneous community or private initiatives that characterize education responses in conflict. In many cases there is a shortage of qualified teachers but a significant demand among the unemployed for teaching positions, especially in urban areas. In the early postconflict period, qualified teachers may be attracted out of the teaching profession to more rewarding opportunities, while large number of unqualified teachers may be drawn into the system, creating a need for both rationalization and professional development. Rationalization of the teaching force rather than recruitment is more often the biggest personnel challenge facing postconflict systems.

Teacher training, often in the form of short courses for teachers, is the activity that engages the widest range of agencies and NGOs. Such training frequently results in a plethora of training courses for teachers, often designed by individual agencies or NGOs and not necessarily targeted to the greatest needs, either in terms of content or geographic distribution. While there is little evidence that these short courses (frequently three to five days) have any measurable impact on teaching practice, experience has shown that they are highly appreciated by the participants for a number of reasons, especially in building teacher morale. The limited evidence available also suggests that programs that are linked to materials production are most likely to have an impact on teaching practice, particularly when supported by follow-up training at the schools.

Facilitating Teacher Return.   During early reconstruction, many teachers return to their previous posts along with members of communities who may have been involved in supporting education during the conflict. Clear guidance on the part of the authorities can help to facilitate the return to school.

- In Kosovo, the UNMIK issued Interim Guidelines for the Resumption of Schooling that provided some guidance to schools authorities on how to deal with teacher appointments on a temporary basis.
- In Timor Leste, the United Nations Transitional Administration in East Timor (UNTAET) managed recruitment of primary teachers through a simple national competency test, although more flexible arrangements had to be made for secondary teachers.

Providing Teacher Support.   Teachers will often return to their posts even when salary systems are not yet in place, but require support as soon as possible, especially in the case of extended conflicts.

- In Kosovo, a system of teacher stipends for teachers in public schools provided motivation for returning teachers even in the absence of a salary system. The stipend system also provided an initial database for the new salary payment system.
- In Timor Leste, a flat salary scale that did not provide for increments permitted rapid implementation of an interim salary system.
- In Sierra Leone, salaries paid by NGOs and international agencies for translators and other staff attracted many teachers away from the profession and generated discontent among teachers and public servants.

Eliminating "Ghost Teachers."   Shortage of qualified teachers is often accompanied by oversupply of underqualified or unqualified teachers in early reconstruction. Poor records can result in "ghost teachers," requiring rationalization of the teaching force.

- In Timor Leste, the selective appointment of primary teachers accompanied by the rapid rise in student numbers resulted in pupil-to-teacher ratios of 52:1.
- In Kosovo, rationalization measures raised the pupil-to-teacher ratio to more sustainable level by eliminating more than 2,000 teaching posts.
- In Sri Lanka, support for teacher rationalization is a key element of World Bank support for education.

- Kosovo, Lebanon, and Sierra Leone all reported problems with "ghost teachers" that had to be eliminated through rationalization and tightening of record-keeping.

Providing Formal Training.   Formal teacher training usually slows or completely stops during conflict, and NGOs can play a helpful role in providing training courses for teachers.

- In Sierra Leone, the International Rescue Committee (IRC) trained teachers in camps but the trainees struggled to get recognition of their qualifications and experience when they returned to the system.
- In Angola, the Jesuit Refugee Service (JRS) trained teachers in National Union for the Total Independence of Angola (UNITA) areas where the government had no access and the rebel forces had failed to display any interest in training teachers.
- The Norwegian Refugee Council (NRC) supported training of teachers in the Uije province in the far north at a time when government officials could not access the area.

Addressing Training Challenges.   Teacher development and training, largely neglected during conflict in most cases, creates particular challenges for postconflict reconstruction as the system has to respond to the training backlog, an influx of untrained teachers, and the limited capacity of the central authorities to coordinate the wide range of private and donor-sponsored training initiatives.

- In Sierra Leone, the Rehabilitation of Basic Education Project provided training for 5,000 teachers.
- In Iraq, where the activity of NGOs was unable to proliferate because of security conditions, all secondary school teachers were given a short course to introduce them to alternative pedagogical approaches
- In Bosnia-Herzegovina, authorities expressed concern that teacher development was driven almost completely by international funding.

The greatest challenge for new authorities is to coordinate this energy into a more coherent teacher development program without stifling it with bureaucratic controls.

- In Kosovo, the UNMIK assigned one agency (the Kosovo Educator Development Program) supported by the Canadian International Development Agency (CIDA) as the "lead agency" responsible for coordinating the very large range of different teacher training initiatives launched by NGOs, agencies, and communities during early reconstruction. This sustained the energy and commitment of teachers and helped to provide a clearer picture of the range of training programs on offer. It also provided a basis for support to the Ministry of Education in developing its teacher training policy.

Involving Teacher Organizations. Teacher organizations, which often have the potential to obstruct reform, can play a significant positive role in supporting reconstruction. The key appears to be in early involvement and ongoing dialogue.

- In El Salvador, teacher unions initially resisted the decentralization of teacher employment that was part of the EDUCO program, but they were encouraged to participate through negotiations.
- In Kosovo, teacher unions, which had played an important role in supporting the parallel system that sustained education for Albanian children for 10 years, initially rejected the stipend system and teacher rationalization strategies employed by UNMIK and managed a series of strikes that disrupted learning. They played a more positive role once they were more directly involved in discussions with the education authorities.

Curriculum Issues

Curriculum and textbook reform requires a cautious and sequential approach to ensure that guidance on key curriculum matters does not outpace development of a wider curriculum vision for the system. The curriculum, which is at the heart of the education system, is the education issue that often generates the highest levels of concern in postconflict contexts.

The curriculum is also at the center of concern over management of diversity in education and in the wider society. Most curricula in the conflict affected countries studied here had either an assimilationist or a separatist approach to dealing with identity, and both of these strategies often become the focus of identity struggles that contribute to conflict. Many sought to move toward a more integrationist approach that would promote greater mutual understanding of cultural and identity difference within a broader framework of tolerance.

Curriculum reform is a major national undertaking requiring strong and clear political leadership, extensive consultations, considerable technical expertise, and comprehensive training programs for teachers. Given that many of these conditions do not exist in postconflict contexts, considerable flexibility and innovation are required to tackle the urgent curriculum issues that confront schools and education authorities. Curriculum reform is strongly conditioned by the extent to which the civil authorities can project a clear vision for education that reflects a broad national consensus. It is a process that proceeds in stages. During the early stages curriculum reform is usually limited to the sanitizing of curricula and textbooks by removing offensive content. Substantive curriculum reform can usually only get underway in later stages of reconstruction, although a number of steps can be taken early to facilitate this process.

Reviewing Textbooks   Textbooks, which often exert more influence on classroom practice than official curriculum documents, are often identified as a starting point for curriculum change, especially where they are seen to reflect bias, prejudice, or distorted accounts.

- In Bosnia-Herzegovina, the three constituent groups reached agreement in 1989 following an elaborate review process on elimination of inappropriate passages from textbooks. However, implementation at the school level has been uneven.
- Sri Lanka constituted a series of respect for diversity review panels that progressively identified problem areas in textbooks.
- With the support of international agencies, UNMIK in Kosovo constituted a panel of local educators to scrutinize existing textbooks for offensive material prior to printing and distribution.
- Within 10 months after the end of conflict in Nicaragua, textbooks from the previous government were destroyed and replaced in every school. In some cases material was copied from neighboring countries' textbooks, which created new problems.
- In Iraq, textbooks distributed to schools in the immediate aftermath of the conflict were reprinted without the pictures of Saddam Hussein or the most obvious symbols of the previous regime; in cases where this was not possible, children were supervised in the tearing out of offensive pictures and pages. In planning for the subsequent year, the Ministry of Education constituted its own panels of teachers and educators to review the textbooks and expurgate the most offensive content.

Implementing Reform Gradually.   Curriculum reform is more effective if implemented gradually in line with the emerging capacity of the education authorities and the national consensus on policy.

- A rapid revision of the curriculum was undertaken as an emergency task in Nicaragua without clarity on principles, goals, and objectives and without altering curriculum architecture.
- Schools in Kosovo operated in the first three years using a range of curricula and textbooks inherited from previous systems and sometimes imported from neighboring countries. A UNICEF-supported team in the education authority received training and support in the development of a curriculum framework that provided the basis for more systematic curriculum development once the provisional government was in power.
- In Kosovo, international support for curriculum development focused on capacity-building for curriculum development institutes and on technical issues like establishing mechanisms for standards and assessment or on training to promote modern pedagogical approaches such as active learning.

Early curriculum reform may involve decisions to eliminate some subjects from the curriculum and to incorporate new issues related to the conflict.

- In Nicaragua, subjects such as political economy were dropped and civics and religious education courses were added to reflect the new government's ideological priorities.
- In Rwanda, agreement was reached to suspend the teaching of history for five years after the conflict.

Revising the Assessment System. Examination and testing systems often wield greater influence over what is taught and learned in class-rooms than the official curriculum documentation. Early reforms that address the assessment system often provide one entry point for curriculum and pedagogical reform. In many cases, the starting point is to build institutional capacity in the assessment system to update concepts of measurement of learning. In Kosovo and Bosnia Herzegovina, early innovations focused on building capacity and consensus on standards and assessment even while the debate continued over curriculum reform.

Financing and Governance

It is prudent to plan for a relatively short-lived "relief bubble" in international financial support that may subside before a more predictable flow of reconstruction resources can be mobilized. Most of the country studies suggest that expectations of a "peace dividend" for education should be modest, given the heavy demand on reconstruction resources from other urgent reconstruction priorities, especially those for economic infrastructure. While data on public expenditure are notoriously difficult to obtain in conflict-affected countries and are often of questionable reliability, figure 5.2 suggests that in cases for which data were available, the share of GDP allocated to education in the year following conflict (or the most recent year in countries emerging from conflict) is rarely any higher than the share allocated in the year prior to conflict. A significant exception was Sierra Leone, where education expenditure was particularly low prior to the conflict. This is one of the few countries where a "peace dividend" seems to have had a significant impact on the education system.

Dealing with Corruption.   Corruption and transparency in education governance are an abiding concern of communities in almost all post-conflict contexts. A constant theme, particularly articulated by communities and parents, in each of the country studies, was corruption or the perception of corruption:

- Distribution and management of education finances
- Awarding of management and teaching posts and admissions
- Examination results
- Promotion to higher grades.

Figure 5.2 Education Expenditure as Percentage of Gross Domestic Product

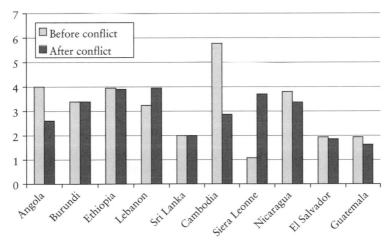

The collapse in public sector salaries often leads to teachers resorting to "extra lessons" for paying students and to other unorthodox practices such as charging "fees" for release of examination results that permit promotion to the next grade.

Once established, the perception of corrupt practices becomes almost impossible to eliminate unless teachers can be paid at a level that permits them to subsist without having to supplement their incomes. Efforts to regulate irregular practices and corruption out of the system such as those tried in Sierra Leone and Cambodia have proved effective only when supported by increased transparency in the allocation of resources and greater control over resources–such as the practice in Cambodian EQIP schools of posting in public the amounts allocated to each school.

Supporting early decisions regarding financing and governance. In some cases the end of conflict brings a significant rush of international financial support to facilitate reconstruction, but in many cases appeals mobilize only a fraction of the resources required. It is rare that international support for recurrent costs can be mobilized for any sustained period, and postconflict reconstruction places heavy demands on public finances from other sectors even as military expenditure declines. Conflict often involves the transfer of a significant share of costs of education to communities and households and to teachers who often have to work for reduced pay, stipends, or incentives. This has impacts on equity of access, on quality of provision, and on teacher morale and motivation. Addressing these issues calls for creative approaches from education authorities emerging from conflict situations.

Accessing Domestic Revenue. Early reconstruction in situations where domestic revenue systems are in disarray presents particular problems and often involves international support for recurrent as well as capital expenditure. Few countries (Iraq may be one exception) have quick access to domestic revenue necessary to keep the system running.

- In Kosovo and Bosnia-Herzegovina, the recurrent costs of the primary and secondary system were covered from domestic revenue within three years, although dependence on international financing for capital development remained high.
- In Timor Leste, projections indicate that recurrent costs will not be covered by domestic revenue for several years, requiring continued support from international sources for recurrent and capital expenditures.
- Nicaragua was able to improve some education indicators during the conflict period in the 1980s, largely through interna-

tional support. El Salvador also benefited significantly from international support in the reconstruction process, a key to its successful recovery.

- In Guatemala and El Salvador, while education expenditure quickly outpaced defense expenditure following the end of conflict, education expenditure as a share of total expenditure still lags behind the regional and global averages, demonstrating that the "peace dividend" for education, although not insignificant, is limited by competition from other sectors.

Linking Support to Long-Term Planning.   International support targeted at reconstruction of infrastructure and other capital investments is more effective when linked to longer-term sector development plans.

- Following the war in Lebanon, almost 30 percent of the education budget was allocated to rehabilitation and reconstruction. When combined with private expenditure on education, some 9 percent of GDP is estimated to have been spent on education in 2000, although 60 percent of this was private spending.
- Social funds in many postconflict countries (such as Bosnia, Cambodia, and Kosovo) provide an important mechanism for targeting resources at community-focused reconstruction programs.
- In Sierra Leone, funds for Heavily Indebted Poor Countries (HIPC) in 2002 will support the rehabilitation of 60 primary and 13 secondary schools, while the REBEP program will cover renovation of 205 primary and 60 secondary schools.

Reducing Household Costs.   Reduction of household costs of education is an effective strategy to promote access and equity that requires careful implementation if it is not to compromise quality.

- Eliminating primary schooling fees and promises of free textbooks in Sierra Leone created significant enrolment growth that outpaced the government's ability to mobilize resources.
- Reducing the household costs of schooling in Timor Leste resulted in significant increases in equity for girls and among poorer and rural households.

Specific Postconflict Challenges

In addition to the "usual business" of system reconstruction, the legacy of conflict brings additional challenges that derive directly from the conflict and call for creative strategies to be integrated into reconstruction programs. The country studies threw limited light and provided only a few examples of creative responses. This brief overview focuses on groups made especially vulnerable by conflict (refugees, internally displaced, child soldiers and war-affected youth, orphans and child-headed households, and disabled persons), on special issues (psychosocial support for students and teachers, peace education and peace-building programs, programs to reduce household and gender-based violence, landmine awareness programs and health and safety messages) and neglected issues (secondary, tertiary, technical/vocational sub-sectors, adult and nonformal education).

Helping the Vulnerable. Postconflict situations usually require additional strategies to respond to the needs of persons with special needs related directly to the conflict, including the following:

- Refugees, internally displaced persons, and returnees place particular demands on education planning at a time when planning capacity and resources are constrained. Frequently conflicts result in substantial urbanization and congestion in urban schools, and populations may not be able or willing to return to rural areas because of safety concerns (such as landmines and residual violence) or, more frequently, for economic reasons. Significant, rapid and unpredictable population movement frequently outpaces conventional planning and school mapping techniques, and calls for more flexible approaches to planning and greater reliance on local initiative.
- The demobilization of child soldiers and other children recruited into service, while not in itself an education challenge, places particular demands on the education system and calls for additional skills and capacity that few schools and teachers have. Some 300,000 young persons under the age of 18 are being exploited as child soldiers in as many as 30 areas of conflict around the world. Successful integration of children and war-affected youth into the education system calls for closer coordination and greater collaboration between the authorities responsible for demobilization and the education authorities.
- Over the past decade, 2 million children were killed in conflict situations, and over 1 million were made orphans.[1] It is increasingly difficult, and not particularly helpful in terms of policy, to differentiate between "conflict orphans" and other orphans, particularly with respect to the fastest growing category–

HIV/AIDS orphans. Children who have lost one or both parents can constitute a substantial proportion of orphans; in Rwanda, in 2000, estimates suggest that some 38 percent of children aged 7–12 had lost one or both parents. Evidence from recent experience suggests that the most important barriers to education participation of orphans in schooling are still the direct and indirect costs. Strategies that address these factors, as well as greater flexibility on age of admission and timetables, have the greatest impact on improving participation of orphans and children from child-headed households.

- Over 6 million children have been seriously injured or permanently disabled by violent conflict over the past decade, and over 10 million have been left with grave psychological trauma. Education systems are rarely able to handle this additional burden and respond adequately even to the needs of children with disabilities not created by conflict. A few examples of creative approaches to addressing the needs of disabled children include the following:
  - Requiring all rehabilitation and major repair contracts for schools to include provision of ramps as part of the rehabilitation work, as in Kosovo.
  - Establishing firm links with local and international advocacy groups for disabled persons, developing a comprehensive policy and strategy for inclusion of children with disabilities into mainstream schools, and supporting the establishment of institutional capacity within the ministry and local authorities.

Addressing Conflict-related Issues. The postconflict context raises issues that schooling is required to address in addition to the regular demands of system reconstruction. Some of the issues identified in the country studies include the following:

- *Psychosocial support* to students to help them recover from stress and trauma experienced in the conflict is often included in education programs. One of the strongest arguments for rapid resumption of schooling (or even schooling during conflict) is that in itself access to school helps establish an atmosphere of normality that builds on children's resilience and assists them in dealing with psychological trauma. Evidence from a number of countries suggests that teachers themselves often require psychosocial support before they can provide assistance to children. Training for teachers can help them provide basic support for children affected by conflict and to acquire the skills to identify and refer children who require support for which teachers are not trained.

- *Peace Education* is a generic term used to describe a range of formal and informal educational activities undertaken to promote peace in schools and communities through the inculcation of skills, attitudes, and values that promote nonviolent approaches to managing conflict and promoting tolerance and respect for diversity. Almost all the country studies contained references to peace education programs undertaken as part of postconflict reconstruction. As yet, however, few evaluations of peace education programs exist.

The Bank-supported initiative in Sierra Leone represents one committed effort to integrate peace education into the curriculum and the system. The Interagency Network on Education in Emergencies (INEE) recently adopted and circulated what is perhaps the most widely used generic package of peace education materials. Some initial lessons that have emerged from the case studies are the following:

- Ill-conceived, stand-alone initiatives emanating from well-meaning outsiders have little positive impact, tend to crowd an already overcrowded curriculum, and collapse as soon as external funding does.
- Peace education initiatives and attempts at forced school integration of alienated communities have limited chances of success.
- Peace education in schools that is linked to wider peace-building in the community is more likely to make an impact on student behavior.
- Programs should focus on a wider range of issues than "peace"–such as life-skills, citizenship, human rights, and health-promotion/HIV/AIDS prevention.
- Attempts at integration of peace education messages "across the curriculum" have been less successful than programs that have a dedicated slot in the curriculum.
- Nonetheless, all curricula should be scrutinized for messages, explicit and implicit, that militate against the inculcation of attitudes of tolerance and acceptance of cultural, ethnic, or religious differences. Such scrutiny is a necessary precursor to peace education programs, which have been shown to be more successful where they combine specific targeted classroom activities with a concern for ensuring that the entire curriculum, formal and hidden, helps to support the messages of the peace education activities.

Supplementary Curriculum Subjects.   In addition to curriculum revision designed to eliminate topics and material that tend to erode social cohesion, the postconflict environment often places additional demands on the curriculum. Circumstances frequently require that landmine awareness and health and safety messages related to postconflict conditions are incorporated into education programs in ways that produce additional demands for more effective intersectoral collaboration and call for skills and training that are not conventionally available to education authorities.

HIV/AIDS and Conflict.   Conflict creates or exacerbates many of the physical, social, and economic conditions and abuse of human rights in which HIV/AIDS flourishes. Population displacement, disintegration of families and communities, rape and sexual abuse, and the collapse of health services are among the factors that make the spread of HIV/AIDS a critical concern for postconflict reconstruction. Poverty and crowded conditions in refugee camps and urban areas increase the risk of sexual violence and prostitution, and armed forces have been identified as having a significantly higher risk of HIV/AIDS infection. The United Nations Children's Fund (UNICEF) reports that of the 25 countries with the highest proportion of children orphaned by AIDS, about one-third have been affected by armed conflict in recent years.

Many of the problems encountered in postconflict system reconstruction, and most of the remedial strategies described here, are familiar to those involved in supporting system development and reform in any education system. The key difference appears to be in the urgency for visible impact in a context where constrained human, financial and institutional resources are complicated by the added burden of massive backlogs and new conflict-related problems. Those authorities that were able to define clear priorities and mobilize the resources of communities, governments and international agencies in a clear and focused way were most likely to deliver on some of the huge expectations that are placed on education systems in such circumstances. Inevitably, choosing priorities means that some issues are neglected. The next chapter reviews some of these neglected issues.

Endnote

1. Office of the Special Representative of the Secretary-General for Children and Armed Conflict. Accessible at http://www.un.org/special-rep/children-armed-conflict/English/Overview.html

CHAPTER 6

Neglected Issues

WHILE THIS STUDY REVEALED a wide range of promising directions and lessons learned in most aspects of education reconstruction, it found little evidence of systematic solutions to a number of largely neglected issues in the countries studied.

Sectoral Imbalance

Basic education was the principal focus of most postconflict reconstruction programs reviewed. An overview of World Bank lending to conflict-affected countries supports this observation. While it is not possible to fully disaggregate all the data according to subsector, the available data on all completed projects in these countries indicates that less than 8 percent was directed specifically to secondary education projects, compared to 43 percent for primary and 12 percent for tertiary education.

This imbalance is not surprising. Primary education is a clear global priority, as reflected in the Millennium Development Goals. Delays in reconstruction of basic education will have long and lasting impacts on the system as a whole. It is also considerably easier to draw on community initiatives and resources in the reconstruction of primary education than in other subsectors. While in most study countries some efforts were also targeted at the secondary and tertiary subsectors and at technical and vocational education, this study uncovered very few examples of innovative approaches to supporting the reconstruction of these critical elements of the education sector.

Yet evidence from the studies suggests that secondary and higher education suffer a more rapid decline during conflict and a more gradual recovery after conflict. Much of the energy and resources of the international community have been directed at basic education, while education authorities have been left to their own resources to deal with the needs of the other subsectors. The result has been that system recovery has in some instances been out of balance in ways that will directly effect economic and social development in the longer term.

The recognition of the need for more balanced responses is growing; examples of multilateral programs that include secondary and tertiary components have increased since 2000. However, the recent experience in Iraq demonstrates the difficulties of mobilizing resources for the secondary and particularly the postsecondary subsectors. While a significant part of the anxiety of the donor community concerns the high unit costs and higher potential for wastage at these levels, the experience in Iraq also points to a recognition that the reform of higher levels of the system is linked more directly to the emergence of a broad development vision for the society. Such a vision often involves political and educational policy choices that interim political and educational authorities are unwilling or unable to make.

Challenges of Interagency Coordination

One of the most significant challenges confronting both international agencies and the national authorities in postconflict contexts concerns interagency coordination. The United Nations has taken significant steps to create mechanisms to coordinate its response better through the Office for the Coordination of Humanitarian Affairs, the network of Humanitarian Coordinators, and the Consolidated Humanitarian Action Plan and Consolidated Appeals Process. Through the creation of its InterAgency Standing Committee (IASC), it has sought to establish better linkages with the leading international nongovernmental organizations (NGOs) working in humanitarian assistance. However, postconflict reconstruction in education involves an interface of humanitarian action and development in direct and complex ways. The result is a plethora of coordination mechanisms that themselves present some challenge in terms of coordination. Figure 6.1 illustrates some of this complexity.

Coordination presents challenges to all development contexts, and perhaps the most important lesson to emerge from global experience is the importance of a strong national authority as the key to effective donor coordination. In a postconflict context, the national authorities are very often not in a solid position to negotiate with international partners, have very limited domestic resources, and frequently consist of new and complex coalitions and interim governance arrangements that makes articulation of a strong national vision difficult. This leads to what Sommers (2004) refers to as a serious imbalance of power, which he describes in some detail in his analysis of interagency coordi-

Figure 6.1 United Nations Coordination Mechanisms
Affecting Education Reconstruction

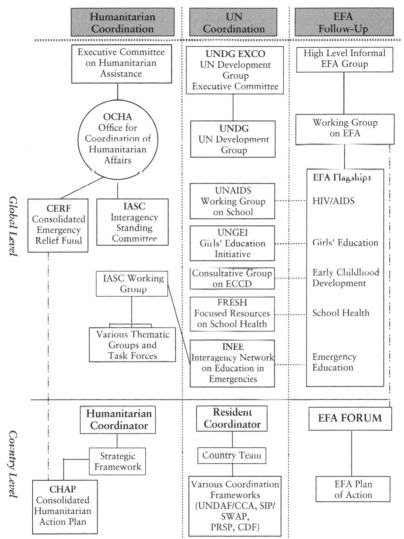

nation. The risks derive from "a general lack of self-examination of
the impact of international agencies during emergencies, and the
tremendous power and influence they can have during and after wars."
The risks he describes may be summarized thus:

In general international agencies may perform the following functions:

- Dominate the setting of educational priorities and policy decisions.
- Demonstrate poor coordination, for example, teacher salary/ incentives are rarely coordinated effectively.
- Effectively limit the geographic distribution of investments, such as the often dramatic difference between investments in education for refugees and internally displaced persons (IDP).
- Restrict the timing of their investments; perhaps most significantly, some donor agencies are restricted from investing, or hesitate to invest substantially, until wars end, which can have serious impacts on the postwar education challenge.
- Control the timing and degree of inclusion of local and national actors.
- Further deplete the capacity of the education system by giving capacity support and development low priority and hiring away many of the most qualified education system personnel.
- Run the risk in some circumstances of effectively becoming "ministries of education" in areas where they operate.

Most of these challenges are clearly manifested in the countries in this study. While there were a few examples of creative strategies to address individual challenges—such as combining the role of Humanitarian and Resident Coordinator or using "lead agencies" and seeking early agreement on salary scales for local staff—it is clear that both effective coordination of agency responses and managing the relationship with existing/emerging civil authorities remain persistent challenges.

Refugees and Internally Displaced Populations

An area of serious neglect that emerged from the study is the question of reintegration of refugees and internally displaced persons into mainstream education systems. The focus of this study was on the provision of education to refugees, which usually takes place during conflict and tends to wind down as conflict subsides and refugees return. There is a growing literature on the education of refugees and a considerable body of experience in provision of education for refugees, especially in refugee camps. This knowledge is best captured in the recently revised United Nations High Commissioner for Refugees UNHCR guidelines for refugee education, in the book that addresses the topic directly (Crisp, Talbot, and Cipolone 2002) and in the many exemplary initiatives that have been written up in the literature. However, as Machel (2001) points out, despite these efforts, fewer than one-third of all refugee schools receive support from outside sources; the majority subsists on its own resources. This results in a lack of coordination of refugee education and especially of education for internally displaced persons. While not the subject of this study, there are some clear trends from refugee education that have significance for postconflict reconstruction:

- The neglect of secondary and postsecondary education typical of postconflict environments is even more pronounced in refugee education. Only six percent of all refugee students are in secondary education. Both in camps and among internally displaced, this creates significant problems in terms of motivation for primary students, supply of teachers for the primary schools, and cohorts of youth who are frustrated, unemployed, and unemployable. Since refugee situations are almost always regarded as temporary arrangements, host governments and donors alike are unwilling to invest significant resources in the more expensive subsectors. Moreover, host governments are often concerned about the politicization of secondary and postsecondary institutions, as well as the possibility of competition for jobs from educated refugees. The most common form of postprimary education provided to refugees is teacher training, which is most common in extended conflicts such as Afghanistan, Burundi, the Democratic Republic of Congo, and Sudan.
- Teachers in refugee camps often develop skills that equip them to make a useful contribution to education on their return. They are more likely to be engaged in curriculum development work, more likely to have experience of multigrade teaching, and often have more exposure to international expertise and alternative pedagogical approaches. Yet upon return to their home countries, they often have difficulties finding employment because of lack of recognition of qualifications and teaching experience.
- While there is general consensus that the ideal curriculum in refugee education is, in principle at least, that of the country of origin, this is frequently not possible. This creates problems of accreditation of learning, especially for returnees who may be forced to re-enter the system at lower levels because prior learning is not recognized. A number of initiatives to develop

internationally accredited programs are being developed but are only in the early stages.

- The medium of instruction and language policy is a particularly sensitive issue for refugee education, especially where they are refugees in a country with a different mother tongue. Teaching in the home language can create problems for refugee youth who seek employment in the country of refuge and can make the education provided in the camps seem irrelevant. However, teaching in the medium of the host country tends to exclude refugee teachers and creates problems for students on their return.

Once postconflict reconstruction begins, refugees and internally displaced persons are viewed for the most part as "returnees" who must be accommodated in the already overcrowded system. Whether, when, and where refugees and displaced persons return can have a very significant impact on postwar education. While few of the systems studied here viewed the refugees as a potential resource, in such countries as Afghanistan, Sierra Leone, and Sudan, returnees often include the best educated students and the most qualified teachers. This has two implications:

- First, the quality of education provided to refugees during conflict and its orientation to the reconstruction of the country of origin can be important factors affecting the reconstruction process. Provision of education to refugees and displaced persons (even during conflict) is a reconstruction and development issue that warrants the attention of agencies committed to reconstruction and development and should not be viewed simply as a humanitarian activity.
- Second, refugees should be viewed more systematically as a resource to education reconstruction rather than as an added burden.

Youth and Adult Education

In almost every country study was the recognition that youth constitute not simply a potential threat to stability should they be recruited into military or criminal activity, but also an important potential resource for development and reconstruction. Yet there were very few examples of practical programs that address the educational needs of youth and young adults. The projects that were included in education reconstruction programs were frequently small in scale and marginalized by the size of the system reconstruction challenge. In many cases ministries consigned nonformal education to NGOs and concentrated their resources and energies on the mainstream schooling system. The concern for education as an important mechanism for building the social cohesion required to ensure lasting peace in postconflict countries rarely manifests itself in substantial programs that address the learning needs of youth.

Limited Initiatives for Lost Learning. The generalized concern about youth and the lack of effective programs to address their needs that was typical of the countries in this study is symptomatic of a growing concern in the international community about the need for more effective policies and strategies for youth. Some limited initiatives were identified. First, accelerated learning programs were designed to attract children who have missed out on years of formal education and provide a compressed curriculum designed to channel them back into the schooling system. Iraq and Sierra Leone were developing such programs, drawing on experiences in Uganda and Liberia for Sierra Leone and in the United States for Iraq. However, this study has had limited success in identifying evaluations of such programs to assess their success.

The second category of programs for youth and young adults who have lost out on schooling opportunities is vocational training. Vocational training presents particular challenges in contexts where resources are constrained and employment opportunities limited, which is frequently the case in postconflict contexts.

Emerging Trends for Youth Education. There is a growing literature on the topic of youth and development and a renewed commitment among many international development agencies, including UNICEF and the World Bank, to a more systematic and strategic approach to the needs of youth, including education. While it is beyond the scope of this study to undertake a detailed review of this literature, it may be helpful for this analysis to point to some of the major trends that are emerging. The first observation is that the needs of youth can only be addressed through a multisectoral framework. As children move through the education system and approach adulthood, it becomes increasingly problematic to compartmentalize into sectors the challenges that youth face, such as education, health, employment, security, and political participation. The difficulty that many governments and agencies have in mounting cross-sectoral programs may be one significant factor in the relatively slow progress that has been made in addressing what has been recognized for decades as a serious need.

Challenges and Opportunities. The main challenges that youth face in postconflict environments, which are similar to those faced by youth in other development contexts, are often exacerbated by conflict and its aftermath. The main challenges and opportunities that emerge from a brief overview of the growing literature on the topic of youth, violence, and postconflict reconstruction can be summarized as follows:

- The most common experience of youth in postconflict reconstruction is one of exclusion (la Cava and Lytle 2004). The slow progress in re-establishing secondary and tertiary educational opportunities, and the marginal status of most adult education programs and accelerated learning opportunities, add to this frustration at a time when involvement in conflict often leaves youth with a new sense of empowerment.
- Exclusion extends to employment, where youth unemployment rates are usually at least double the national rate. In Kosovo, more than 60 percent of youth were unemployed two years after the conflict; similar patterns can be found in almost all countries studied. It is also clear that youth are disproportionately represented among those employed in the informal sector.
- Exclusion also extends to political marginalization and exclusion from participation in decisionmaking, both in their own education and in wider political processes.
- Youth are most frequently associated with violence and crime in postconflict contexts. There is some concern in the literature that these negative aspects of youth tend to attract most public and policy attention, rather than the positive contribution that many youth are making to social and economic reconstruction. Evidence from many countries suggests that, where violent conflict subsides, failure to address the needs of youth results in a growth in youth involvement in violence and crime. The cases of El Salvador and South Africa, where violent crime and gang activity has mushroomed in urban areas since the end of the war, illustrate this trend.
- An associated trend in the literature is the issue of urbanization. Marc Sommers' recent study of urbanization, war, and youth at risk in Africa describes a central irony of African youth: "[T]hey are a demographic majority that sees itself as an outcast minority" (2003, p.1). The attractions of the city that draw youth from the rural areas are exacerbated in a postconflict environment by the official neglect of rural areas that is typical of early reconstruction.

- Youth are also particularly vulnerable to health and safety hazards typical of a postconflict environment, especially with respect to HIV/AIDS.

Interlinked Initiatives

Education is frequently identified as one of the strategies required to address the challenges confronting youth in post conflict societies, but it is clear from the nature of the challenges that it can only be effective if it is part of a combination of interlinked initiatives. This added complexity accounts to a certain extent for the limited number of successful programs for youth in postconflict societies. Some key strategies were identified:

- Inclusion and empowerment of youth, which has implications for the way youth are involved in influencing what happens inside schools and colleges, as well as for their participation in developing the range of programs designed to address youth issues.
- Support for employment and income-generation programs that offer incentives and sources of startup financing to encourage youth entrepreneurship imply more flexibility in curriculum choice and a wider range of options that will permit youth to develop the requisite skills. Sommers (2003) summarizes some of the most effective strategies in Box 6.1.

  Skills training for youth is seriously under-resourced in most postconflict contexts (Sesnan and others 2004). Experience suggests that schools are ill-equipped to provide effective training in practical skills, but the emerging body of work on "livelihood skills" as part of "life skills" may offer some direction for education systems. Practical training courses that meet needed skills are most effectively provided by the private sector or by NGOs. Youth-targeted health, education, and social protection interventions to help youth avoid risky behaviors require creative approaches, including peer education programs.

The Role of Private Education

The distinction between private and public provision becomes blurred in postconflict contexts, when community efforts to carry on functions formerly provided by the state overlap with initiatives of churches,

---

Box 6.1 Strategies that Address Youth Unemployment and Exclusion

- Target the marginalized youth majority.
- Design emphatically inclusive programs.
- Actively encourage female youth participation.
- Develop holistic programs.
- Draw from existing entrepreneurial skills for vocational training.
- Foster trust by providing access to capital.
- Create effective networks with existing youth programs.
- Maintain ongoing program evaluations and revisions.

Source: Sommers 2003.

NGOs, and other civil society interests. One trend noted in the country studies was the tendency for community and private schools to be less affected by the ravages of conflict than those more closely identified with the state. Systems that that had formerly discouraged private schooling often witness in the postconflict era a resurgence of private initiatives, but the data available to this study did not permit a systematic analysis of the ways in which private schooling interacted with the reconstruction of the system, largely because data on private schooling is frequently unavailable or unreliable. The Lebanese experience, where schooling was predominantly private before and after the conflict, illustrates both the strengths and the limitations of a predominantly private system. Few other case studies offer enough evidence of the way various levels of private ownership and control can contribute to, or undermine, the reconstruction of education.

In Haiti, which has faced the legacy of decades of recurring conflict and civil unrest, 80 percent of schools (75 percent primary, 82 percent secondary) schools were privately owned (World Bank 1998). The private sector catered to an elite with privileged and well-resourced schools, and to the poor majority, leaving public schools to service the small largely urban middle class. Fewer than 10 percent of private schools were licensed by the state. As it struggles with the challenges of postconflict reconstruction Haiti faces two critical questions regarding private education. First, it needs to substantially increase public expenditure on education in a way that builds on the strengths of the private system rather than simply expands public schooling. Second, it is wrestling with the challenge of introducing regulation of the private education sector, without introducing bureaucratic controls that will further impede the provision of quality education by both public and private schools. A range of strategies that channel public resources to private education within a well-regulated framework are among the options facing Haiti.

The issues discussed in this chapter are neglected in two senses. They tend to receive little attention and a smaller share of resources in humanitarian assistance and postconflict reconstruction programs, and there is a very limited commitment to research for better understanding of the problems. At the same time, they are repeatedly identified as areas that warrant greater attention and resources.

References

Crisp J., Talbot C., and Cipolone D., eds. *Learning for a Future: Refugee Education in Developing Countries.* United Nations High Commissioner for Refugees, Geneva.

la Cava, Gloria, and Paula Lytle. 2004. "Youth–Strategic Directions for the World Bank." Draft discussion paper prepared for ECSSD. World Bank, Washington, D.C.

Machel, G. 2001. *The Impact of War on Children.* London: Longman Ltd.

Sesnan B., G. Wood, M. Anselme, and A. Avery. 2004. "Skills Training for Youth." *Forced Migration Review* 20 (May): 33–35.

Sommers, M. 2003. "Urbanization, War and Africa's Youth at Risk." USAID, Washington, D.C. http://www.beps.net/publications/BEPS-Urbanization WarYouthatRisk.pdf.

World Bank. 1998. "Haiti: the Challenges of Poverty Reduction, Vol. One." PREM and Caribbean CMU Report 17242-HA. World Bank, Washington, D.C.

CHAPTER 7

A Role for the World Bank

THE END OF THE COLD WAR signaled a significant change in the nature of conflicts, with a substantial increase in civil war as opposed to interstate conflicts. This development has led the World Bank to progressively review and adapt its approach to postconflict reconstruction. The World Bank has been involved in postconflict reconstruction since its inception as the International Bank for Reconstruction and Development. It is, however, prohibited by its Articles from becoming involved in humanitarian relief, for which other agencies have a specific mandate. There has been fairly rapid progress recently in thinking through the Bank's role in postconflict reconstruction generally, including linkages to Comprehensive Development Frameworks (CDF), Poverty Reduction Strategy Papers (PRSP), and Heavily Indebted Poor Countries (HIPC).[1] In addition to this review of the relationships between conflict and wider development frameworks, poverty reduction, and debt relief, important work has been undertaken on the framework of Low Income Countries Under Stress (LICUS).

Equally significant has been a shift of focus from postconflict reconstruction to conflict prevention, of which reconstruction is but one key element. This is reflected in the change of name of the former Post Conflict Unit to the Conflict Prevention and Reconstruction Unit (CPRU). In addition to its monitoring role and support to conflict-affected countries, the CPRU has led the development of tools such as the Conflict Analysis Framework (CAF). The Bank's support for education in conflict-affected countries has increased in both scale and scope as the new operational policies are implemented.

A recent review of World Bank engagement from the client's perspective stresses that the "Bank is never as true to its original mission as when it is engaged in post-conflict reconstruction" (Colletta and Tesfamichael 2003, p. 2). The report suggests that the main areas where Bank engagement is critical are as follows:

- Macroeconomic stabilization and growth, which require more careful consideration of the sociopolitical realities of the postconflict context, and a combination of support for large-scale infrastructure investments as well as small and medium enterprises

- Governance, institutional reform, and capacity-building, including support for government in managing expenditures better with greater public oversight and transparency
- Collaboration, coordination, and implementation, including more effective donor coordination, better conflict analysis with community participation, and more effective partnerships.

Deployment of Bank Resources

Table 7.1 and figure 7.1 present an analysis of expenditures on completed or active Bank projects in the conflict-affected countries included in this study. The analysis yielded a total expenditure of approximately US$1 billion in 21 countries. Of this, 40 percent was spent on activities to "improve access," a similar share committed to "quality improvements," and 14 percent on management reforms and capacity-building In the category of "Quality," the biggest single item was textbooks and materials (US$231million), followed by teacher training (US$78 million). Funds for increasing access were dominated by US$230 million on physical construction and rehabilitation activities. Management reforms included US$60 million on policy and management development, including work on sector reform strategies, and US$73 million on institutional strengthening, mostly in the form of management training. This suggests that in terms of financial mobilization, the greatest areas of World Bank involvement to date have been in construction and textbooks, with significant expenditures on management reforms and capacity-building.

However, the size of the expenditure does not necessarily fully reflect the significance of the investment. More of the currently active projects and more of the more projects initiated since 1998 have a greater share committed to management and policy development and institutional strengthening, although construction and textbooks remain by far the largest areas of investment. The study identified a number of promising directions for World Bank involvement:

- *Use the framework of prevention, transition, and recovery offered in the World Bank Operation Policy "Development Cooperation and Conflict" OP2.30 as a basis for more flexible approaches to postconflict reconstruction.* The framework and the more flexible operational procedures in Operational Policy

Table 7.1 Analysis of World Bank Loan and Grant Education
Expenditure (Completed and Active) in 21 Conflict-Affected
Countries, 1994–2002

<<$'000
okay?>>

Area	Focus	$'000	%
Quality	Curriculum	65.5	6.8
	Teacher training	78.6	8.2
	Student assessment	10.8	1.1
	Monitoring service delivery	8.8	0.9
	Textbooks and libraries	231.1	24.0
	Other	10.0	1.0
	Total	404.6	42.1
Access	Distance learning	5.9	0.6
	Improving access	156.4	16.3
	Construction and rehabilitation	230.1	23.9
	Other	2.0	0.2
	Total	394.4	41.0
Education	Management and		
Management	policy development	60.0	6.2
	Institution strengthening	73.8	7.7
	Other	0.3	0.0
	Total	134.13	13.9
	Project management		
	and implementation	28.6	3.0
Total		961.65	100.0

Total Bank Spending on Education Projects in Conflict Countries since 1994

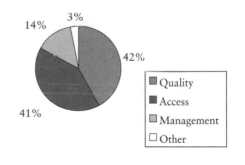

14%   3%

42%

41%

- Quality
- Access
- Management
- Other

"Emergency Recovery Assistance (OP8.50) provide a practical basis for more streamlined and efficient progress in responding to crisis and conflict. However, the emphasis of World Bank projects still tends to be on transition and recovery. The concept of prevention needs to be built more systematically into the instruments and analyses that are part of every Bank engagement, so that sensitivity to conflict becomes a basic component of the way the Bank works. The regulations and policies are in place, but a wider recognition by country directors and task managers of the critical links among conflict, poverty, and education, as well as of the potential role of education in conflict prevention, would help to ensure a stronger focus on conflict prevention fundamental approach to development challenges.

- *Participate more actively in global collaboration for country-level coordination.* At the global level there has been significant progress since April 2000 when the education ministers of 24 conflict-affected countries requested the three agencies of the United Nations most closely associated with education in "emergencies"—the United Nations Childrens Fund (UNICEF), United Nations High Commisioner for Refugees (UNHCR), and United Nations Education Scientific and Cultural Organisation (UNESCO)—to lead an initiative in promoting greater international coordination. The Interagency Network on Education in Emergencies (INEE), established in November 2000 at a Consultative Meeting mandated by the Dakar World Education Forum, quickly established that a plethora of "coordination mechanisms" established to promote better interagency coordination in emergency education responses already exists. Figure 6.1 (page 65) suggests that these mechanisms exist to promote coordination at both global and country level within each coordination focus (humanitarian assistance, development cooperation, and Education for All [EFA]) but that there is limited provision for coordinating linkages between them. One exception is the INEE, which has institutional linkages to both the humanitarian assistance community—through the Inter Agency Standing Committee (IASC) Working Group—and to the EFA. World Bank participation as an active member in such global partnerships can help to ensure its involvement in supporting and influencing the direction of global coordination efforts.

Significant progress has been made recently through the IASC and United Nations Development Group (UNDG) to more closely align the mechanisms and instruments used. Closer alignment would facilitate the possibility of a smoother transition from humanitarian assistance and reconstruction and development, partly through the mechanism of the Consolidated Humanitarian Action Plan (CHAP) that is increasingly integrated into the Consolidated Appeals Process (CAP). Through the Fast Track Initiative (FTI) and other initiatives there has been significant progress in unifying the EFA plans with both education sector plans and with wider development frameworks offered by the HIPC process and PRSP.

The World Bank, which has a presence in the IASC, is increasingly involved in early reconstruction collaboration, such as the recent United Nations Development Group/World Bank Joint Needs Assessment on Iraq. Through its representation in the INEE, the World Bank can help to promote a better appreciation within that global network of the reconstruction continuum from prevention through crisis to development.

Within the World Bank itself, the Education Hub, as the coordinator of knowledge sharing, can play a more active role in alerting country directors and task managers to the critical role that the Bank can play in ensuring that the lessons learned in one region are shared and reflected on by colleagues in other regions—not simply in countries facing obvious conflict challenges. The shift of focus to conflict prevention also suggests value in studying countries where social conflict has not led to violence, to establish what lessons can be shared both with those engaged in postconflict reconstruction and other countries where education systems may be unwittingly stoking the fire of social discord. The World Bank brings a particular set of competencies and skills that no other multilateral agency can bring to postconflict reconstruction with the same authority and should continue to provide leadership in such areas as the following:

- *Enhance sector analysis and linkage to wider development policies.* The World Bank's key role—expertise in sector work, development, and economic analysis and access to wider development planning processes—position it well to play a central role in building links among education sector development plans and the Comprehensive Development Plans, PRSPs, and Interim PRSPs, and assisting conflict affected countries to qualify for HIPC relief.
- *Develop more flexible approaches to Analytic Advisory Activities (AAA) and Economic and Sector Work (ESW) so that it can be more iterative in nature.* The contribution of analyses of public expenditure, poverty studies, and sector reviews to

reconstruction would be facilitated if such studies could be undertaken in a more iterative manner, so that early findings could be built on in subsequent analyses as data and access improve.

- *Conduct planning for early reconstruction while conflict and humanitarian relief dominate international response.* Since the World Bank is not permitted by its Articles to engage in humanitarian relief, it can focus its energies during conflict and humanitarian relief on doing preparatory work, data collection for rapid assessment missions, sector analysis, and work on key technical issues to permit rapid progress on reconstruction.

- *Provide direct support to development of policy options, strategies, technical tools, and capacity-building in the area of system financing and governance.* While most agencies direct their energies to the immediate practical problems of restarting the education system, the World Bank is well positioned to support work on financial decentralization and management, school and system governance, and legal and regulatory frameworks that help to facilitate the transition from crisis interim arrangements to a sustainable and accountable system.

- *Provide expertise in intersectoral areas that other more specialized agencies may not be as well positioned to address.* The country studies demonstrate that the nature of postconflict reconstruction makes effective intersectoral collaboration particularly urgent. Education systems need to collaborate across sectors on HIV/AIDS programs, health education, safety and security in schools, landmine awareness, and psychosocial support. Community involvement and the key role of social funds in reconstruction require effective linkages among ministries that the Bank is well positioned to support. Support for teacher policies requires interfacing with civil service authorities, finance ministries, and social welfare and pensions departments. All these areas can benefit from the broad intersectoral expertise that the World Bank is able to mobilize.

- *Ensure that conflict-affected countries are supported in their development planning to become part of the EFA planning and Fast Track Initiative (FTI).* Of the 52 countries involved in conflict since 1990 that were identified for this study, 18 (35 percent) are rated by the World Bank as "on-track" for EFA, four have already achieved Universal Primary Completion (UPC), and the remaining 14 have been assessed as on track to do so by 2005. Of the 20 "on-track" countries, eight are in the Europe and Central Asia Region, and only one is in Sub-Saharan

Africa. The list of 52 conflict-affected countries includes eight that have been invited to submit proposals for the FTI, of which two (Democratic Republic of Congo and Pakistan) are on the Analytical Fast Track (AFT). The World Bank should work with its development partners to ensure that the EFA movement and the energy and resources mobilized by the FTI help to close the gap between conflict-affected countries and other countries.

- *Engage in Knowledge Sharing.* The World Bank has a key role in sharing knowledge on programs and strategies that address postconflict reconstruction, both with governments and development partners in countries and through wider knowledge networks such as the INEE.

- *Consolidate data for conflict-affected countries.* This study revealed that in those conflict-affected countries in which the World Bank is operational, the data from its expenditure reviews, sector studies, Living Standards Measurement Surveys (LSMS), and other social sector assessments constitute a valuable source of information in contexts where even basic data are often extremely limited and of dubious quality. The Bank could play a valuable role in ensuring that data collected in these countries in which it is operational are made more widely available, both within the countries and with international partners and the UNESCO Institute for Statistics (UIS).

Neglected Areas of Youth and Secondary Education

This study has identified a number of areas where little work has been done on developing strategies that address the particular conditions of postconflict reconstruction. In many cases these areas receive less attention in the early years of reconstruction; when they are addressed, the proffered solutions tend to be in terms that do not take into account the postconflict environment. Among these are the following:

- *Provide leadership in secondary education.* Available data suggest that the share of resources to secondary education declines in immediate postconflict years, although enrollment rates expand rapidly. Of the US$1 billion spent on education projects in conflict countries since 1994, only 8 percent was specifically targeted to secondary education programs, while 46 percent was specifically for primary and 12 percent specifically for tertiary programs. The balance was allocated to programs that affected all subsectors. Given the generally low level of support for secondary education, the growing involvement of the World Bank in secondary education more widely, the Bank may be well positioned to provide more active leadership and support for secondary education in postconflict reconstruction.

- *Develop initiatives to help key constituencies.* The situation of war-affected youth, demobilized soldiers, and young people who have not completed basic education was a recurring concern in the countries studied, and yet there are relatively few examples of initiatives that target this key constituency and few lessons to derive.

- *Develop criteria for World Bank involvement in education activities.* OP 3.20 provides a basis for determining the level of Bank engagement in countries affected by conflict. However, the emphasis on early involvement, as well as the complex relationship among education, social cohesion, and conflict, suggest that some supplementary guidance may be helpful with respect to education activities. In addition to the broad framework of principles articulated earlier, the following three may provide a starting point for such criteria:

  1. The first consideration should be for safety, not only of Bank staff but also of students, teachers, and officials. There are examples where gathering children and teachers together make them more vulnerable to recruitment or attack.
  2. Support for education activities should not support indoctrination or further widen disparities that contribute to conflict.
  3. Bank support for education should build on and enhance the delivery capacity of local communities, authorities, and other agencies already active in supporting education rather than compete with them.

- *Revisit the range of operational activities supported by the Bank during conflict and the transition to early reconstruction.* OP3.20 provides a broad framework for Bank involvement in countries affected by conflict. However, this study emphasizes the significance of early involvement in education as a development activity even as humanitarian assistance is the predominant basis for international support. This may involve elaborating on the "Watching Brief" activities to include support for education initiatives that prepares the ground for reconstruction, helps to preserve valuable system assets such as information systems and education data, and supports early initiatives to pilot approaches in safe areas that may serve as a resource of experience and expertise.

- *Balance support for physical reconstruction and supply of learning materials with activities that help prepare the ground for reconstruction.* These activities include research on legal and regulatory frameworks, capacity-building for key institutions and planning infrastructure (such as EMIS and teacher and curriculum development institutes and centers, and standards and assessment capacity), and development of policy options for system decentralization and/or recentralization.
- *Recognize the importance of sequencing of responses according to the priorities of reconstruction, which may be influenced by political, educational, and social considerations as well as by logistical ones.* These factors will be context-specific but may involve, for instance, weighing the value of early investment in repair and rehabilitation to provide early evidence of visible impact against the risk of relapse into violence and the subsequent destruction of such infrastructure.
- *Promote the use of grants and innovative funding mechanisms such as the Trust Funds used in Afghanistan and Timor Leste to initiate reconstruction activities.* The analysis of education loans and grants since 1994-2001 lists only three education grants to conflict affected countries amounting to less than $26 million out of a total of more than $1 billion. The need for rapid and flexible action in postconflict contexts would be met by more direct use of grant funds, such as the recent IDA grant to Kosovo, and more recently the US$100 million in grants for education projects from the World Bank Iraq Trust Fund. The succession of funding mechanisms that has been associated with many successful initiatives starts from early use of Trust Funds (such as the Post Conflict Fund), through special multiagency trust funds (such as those established in Afghanistan, Timor Leste, and, more recently, Iraq), to IDA grants and credits. Other Bank instruments, such as the Adaptable Program Lending (APL), Learning and Innovation Loans (LIL), and Economic Recovery Credit (ERC) have been quite extensively used in postconflict contexts.

The combination and sequencing of Bank services requires close attention. The evidence from this study points to the importance of the Bank being able to mobilize significant resources for the major reconstruction process, where it often plays a lead role in mobilizing or channeling resources for reconstruction. Recognizing this key role means also emphasizing the importance of early investment in AAA work and Technical Assistance (TA) to provide the basis for subsequent grant or lending operations, in capacity-building to ensure the local capacity to negotiate, manage, and monitor large projects, and in knowledge sharing.

- *Focus more systematically on the private sector, training, and market aspects of education.* No other agency is as well placed as the World Bank to work at this interface. This could involve earlier and more systematic involvement of other parts of the World Bank Group, such as Multilateral Investment Guarantee Agency (MIGA) and International Finance Corporation (IFC).

Endnote

1. For example, OP2.30 Operational Policies: Development Cooperation and Conflict (2001); or World Bank (1998). "The World Bank's Experience with Post-Conflict Reconstruction," Operations Evaluation Department, World Bank, Washington D.C; and, of course, "Post Conflict Reconstruction: The Role of the World Bank" (1998), World Bank, Washington, D.C. See also reports to the Development Committee on "Assistance to Post-Conflict Countries and the HIPC Framework" (2001) and "Review of the PRSP Approach" (2002:10–11).

Reference

Colletta, N.J., and G. Y. Tesfamichael. 2003. "Bank Engagement After Conflict: A Client Perspective." A background document for the Post-Conflict Workshop in Maputo, July 17-18. World Bank, Washington, D.C.

CHAPTER 8

Concluding Comments

THIS REVIEW OF EXPERIENCE of education and postconflict reconstruction offers a partial perspective on a complex and intricate set of problems. The mushrooming of analyses, publications, and research projects that examine this issue points to a growing recognition that education has an essential role both in promoting or preventing conflict, and as a fundamental element of wider social and economic reconstruction. The bulk of these analyses suggest an increased appreciation for the importance of early investment in education as a necessary initial step in postconflict reconstruction. The recognition that education systems are almost always complicit in conflict, that they rarely completely cease to function, and that they rapidly resume operations with or without outside support as violence subsides is an important factor responsible for this growing interest in early education response. Without reform, reconstruction runs the danger of reproducing the factors that contributed to the conflict in the first place. Postconflict societies face the extraordinary demands of simultaneous reconstruction and reform. The context offers both opportunities for change and the challenges of an extremely complex and demanding environment.

One of the strongest factors conditioning postconflict reconstruction and setting it apart is a pervasive sense of urgency. Yet peace building is a long-term activity. Education systems and schools provide only one of the key institutional networks for peacebuilding, and what is possible and effective in building peace in the wider society conditions (and is conditioned by) what is possible and effective in schools. This powerful tension between the need for urgent changes in the way schools work and the slow and often tortuous process of peacebuilding has created an even stronger appreciation of the importance of sequencing of education responses.

The concern about time and sequencing adds layers of complexity to the challenge of prioritization. As this study illustrates, education reconstruction and reform present wide-ranging and often competing demands in a context with significant resource constraints–human, institutional, and social, as well as economic and financial. The more effective responses are those that have been able to move rapidly and strategically to balance the urgent and the important. While there are no simple formulae or cookie-cutter approaches, the lessons from experience show the value of focusing on the basics while making a commitment to address the full range of issues over time and in a clearly prioritized sequence.

The lessons underscore the importance of ensuring that there is sufficient evidence of early and visible progress to sustain popular support for the peace process, for the education authorities, and for the reform process. The study highlights the value of early investment in sector work that will provide a basis for subsequent reforms and will expedite the development of a national vision for education reform that is the key both to continued popular support and coordination of international agencies.

Education does not cause wars, nor does it end them. It does, however, frequently contribute to the factors that are underlie conflict, but it also has the potential to play a significant role both directly and indirectly in building peace, restoring countries to a positive development path, and reversing the damage wrought by civil war.

Index